EVERY WILLING HAND

COMMUNITY, ECONOMY AND EMPLOYMENT

SHAMCHER BRYN BEORSE

℘

THE SHAMCHER ARCHIVES

ALPHA GLYPH PUBLICATIONS

Every Willing Hand: Community, Economy and Employment

© 1979 Bryn Beorse and © 2014 The Shamcher Archives
Introduction © 2014 by Carol Sill
Cover Design: Diane Feught
Song quotation: Every Willing Hand,
Words and music ©Carol Ann Sokoloff, SOCAN

Library and Archives Canada Cataloguing in Publication

Beorse, Bryn, 1896-1980, author
    Every willing hand : community, economy and
employment / Shamcher Bryn Beorse.

Originally published: New York : Hu Press, 1979.
ISBN 978-0-9783485-4-0 (pbk.)

    1. Conduct of life. 2. Beorse, Bryn, 1896-1980. 3. Free choice of
employment. 4. United States--Economic policy--1971-1981. I. Title.

BJ1581.2.B46 2014   191   C2014-902859-8

www.every-willing-hand.shamcher.com

Alpha Glyph Publications Ltd
Vancouver BC Cannada

"Every willing hand, shall be put to service
Here we take our stand, no one to be worthless.."
- Carol Ann Sokoloff

Contents

Introduction

hrough *Every Willing Hand* we can receive a glimpse of an extraordinary worldview, a simultaneous multiverse of intimate interconnection, fueled by love, aligned by wisdom, creatively expressing God's love for this delicate and persistent human experiment. This is the world of Shamcher Bryn Beorse.

With this book Beorse views this vast scene through a lens of economics and full employment. He reveals artfully interwoven themes that all work together to show a complex picture of the forces and influences at play, both at the time of writing in the mid-1970's and today. Shamcher had great compassion for those who are "half awake in the body of humanity," and he worked tirelessly to expand the horizons of all individuals and communities.

In one glance the book reflects innumerable facets of our social communities and individual aspirations, all in the context of the need for social reform. Where does he suggest this reform comes from? Not from a revolution in the streets to restore or establish fair and equal opportunity, but from an implemented program ensuring full employment for all who want it. A program that had already been outlined back in 1946 by noted economist, John H. G. Pierson.

An economist himself, Beorse adds his voice to Pierson's concept in his own inimitable way: by providing this swirling overview of the issues at hand, ranging from the personal to the cosmic.

A key to discovering the meaning of this book is to approach it visually. I invite you to see the whole book as a Diego Rivera-style mural. As in a mural, at one view all the major public figures and social influences can be seen interacting together symbolically on a wall in a public place. Time past, present and future are all represented. Such a mural can be understood by anyone. It is always a call to action, a statement of deep participation in life in our community, an acknowledgement of roots in the past, the reality of present problems and hope for the future.

Like any great muralist, Beorse includes specific significant details: some informational for future reference, some symbolic for contemplation. While reading this book, visualizing is key to comprehensive understanding. Taking the time to think and contemplate may open catalysts to insight and give inspiration for action. Let's take a look at the vast mural that is *Every Willing Hand*.

The first chapter, *Every Single Willing Hand*, introduces the book's purpose, touching on economics, full employment, and OTEC (Ocean Thermal Energy Conversion). Beorse introduces the influential figures whose ideas form a basis for this discussion, including thinkers and economists who by now may have faded from the world stage. We can't ignore the fact that this book began with a memory: the suicide of a talented man, whose enthusiasm and gifts were suppressed by his involuntary unemployment.

Children's Hour uses the future generation as an inspiration for action, asking "what do the children of unemployed workers feel and think?" then leading directly into correspondence that reveals the efforts to create new initiatives. Moving from child to youth, in *The Unsettled*, he first asks the question, "How can youth build a viable society when unsettled?" His response includes the work of the esteemed Dr. Ménétrier in his Paris clinic, and touches on inner guidance and the "unseen friend".

Generation Bridge, written at the time of the "generation gap" offers new approaches to gaps in understanding between any groups whose concepts and theories differ. While touching on teachings of the sufis, including yoga and meditation, a great deal of this chapter is devoted to Dr. Simonton's work using visualization with cancer patients. If visualization is proven to help in individuals, can it not also be a clue to helping our communities, and our future?

The next chapter, *Vendettas and Morality*, takes another look at our society, from marriage to long term social planning, and the negative influence of unemployment. Here Beorse posits employment based on enthusiasm and skills, not merely abilities in reading and writing. *The Good Samaritan and Computers* outlines a very interesting juxtaposition. He states, "Computers, lie detectors and good Samaritans sway people, their communities, economics." Here he shows us how the help of a caring human being restores the humanity in others, for in many ways we are being "beaten up" by the media and our dependence on the external. Incidentally, Beorse saw lie detectors as machines that measured feeling, and as such creating a whole new category of social influence that will emerge in the future.

Like his teacher, the Sufi Hazrat Inayat Khan, Shamcher had an intuitive awareness of the power and meaning of symbols. In *A Symbol is an Ocean in a Drop,* he examines the Cross, the Trinity, the Waters of the Sea, Bread, and Wine. This chapter is an entrance to the world of the spirit. It looks at concentration, prayer, and most important: developing an understanding of the physical aspects of thoughts and feelings. Stepping further into the mystic world, *Communicators* introduces examples of those who could operate beyond the limitations of body and mind. The figures of Inayat Khan, Samuel Lewis, Rabindranath Tagore, Dag Hammarskjold, and Al Ghazali appear to our view.

And then, *War.* Seeing from the economic viewpoint, Beorse gives a global overview, mentioning how economic despair opened the door to Hitler. He offers the choice of full employment and its related economic stability as a potential deterrent to future wars. In *Riots: A Challenge?* Shamcher significantly asks if riots come from ourselves, from "a mysteriously expanded multimind." Invoking history, he describes riots and demonstrations as warnings to communities to take stock of assets and potentialities.

From war and riots, to we turn to love, and in *Love, How Real?* love is shown as a realization, as the basis for a society and its economics. From the human cycle of love to the love of God, this chapter reveals the stream of love in its many forms. Then from such a Bhakti yoga approach, the next chapter flows to a more Jnana approach. *"I Am Just An Accident"* takes a scientific view, contrasting "a" and "b" in a conversational dialogue between two characters, Ralph and

Fred, a biologist and an astrophysicist.

Is there a way out? *Freedom's Gate* begins with a well-known Sufi story, then goes right into the main teaching this story reveals: die before death. Shamcher shows the path of forgetting the self, losing the self in the wonder of Creation. All clashes and differences can be united in prayer. The chapter *Clashing Minds* decodes prayers with concentrations for each line of the *Lord's Prayer*, and two Sufi prayers, including this healing prayer:

Beloved Lord, Almighty God
Through the Rays of the Sun
Through the Waves of the Air
Through the All-Pervading Life in Space
Purify and revivify us, and we pray,
Heal our bodies, hearts and souls.

Looking at states and stages of realization, this chapter shows prayer, meditation and contemplation as essential tools of education.

In *Silent Reach* Shamcher goes much further into breath, yoga, Sufism, inner training and practice. He defines the seeker as an astronaut, stepping outside narrow mind, feelings and body into wide open space. This approach gives access to the solutions to all our social, economic, international and personal problems and ambitions.

Those solutions remain unfulfilled until they are applied, and that is where the work needs to be done. So from meditation and inner life it is back to *That Unfinished Business* where the book first began. Back to economics, and to the ideas of inventory, surveys and analysis to lay the groundwork for full employment. Here Beorse mentions the comprehensive 1963 meeting that had been planned to hammer out such basics for the US, a meeting that was tragically cancelled due to the assassination of President Kennedy. However, further correspondence included here indicates that the ideas behind this meeting were still in play.

This business is still unfinished, which is why Beorse wrote this book. For those who want further details, the Appendix contains the full statement *Completing the Employment Act* by John H.G. Pierson, as presented to the US House of Representatives in 1972.

This book is not only historical but completely in the present. Perhaps now could be the time to look back at the 1946 proposal for full employment. It is certainly not too late to examine the work of the economists Beorse so emphatically recommends. Nor is it too late to advocate the implementation of OTEC technology for the good of our planet, climate and economy. And now is always the right time to develop the inner life. As outlined in *Silent Reach*, we can all expand ourselves to become explorers who step outside narrow mind and concepts, and enter wide open space.

Carol Sill, Vancouver 2014

Every Single Willing Hand

Aroaming tramp who had seen a man hang himself because nobody wanted his labor and enthusiasm - broke off his stay abroad and hastened home when young, perceptive John F. Kennedy entered the White House. Here, thought our traveler (my unhumble self), is a man who thinks, and who cares.

Two secret service men grilled me in a corner of the lobby of the All-State Hotel, or rather, one grilled me; the other looked me sternly and silently over from the side. He had a livid scar across his face, suggesting to me that he was ready for any type of action that might become required. The other guests ogled the threesome with apprehension.

When the ordeal was over, I felt that general civilities required a few polite words to the silent partner.

"In 1940," I offered, "a German military intelligence agent, Lieutenant Khul, also looked me over silently like you did. I believe be thought he could read my mind. He hardly could. But I have no doubt that you could, and did."

He came through with a brief response, "Thank you." There was no smile.

When cleared, I telephoned the White House and a voice answered, "I am Paul Black (not his real name), can I help you?"

When Paul heard my errand, clumsily presented, he exploded.

"You cannot see anybody in the White House, now or ever, do you understand?"

"I am not sure I do, Mr. Black."

A question to the communicative secret service man produced a terse, "Paul obviously has grown too big for his britches. Would you wait a minute at the phone?"

A few seconds later came a well-modulated voice, "This is Arthur Schlesinger. Care to come over at eleven?"

Thus began a three year long labor of love with an ever expanding group of Administration economists, historians, planners, farmers and computer nuts. Our goal was simple: continuous full employment for every willing hand.

At the time of the Founding Fathers, employment was a matter of course. A continent was to be developed. Enterprising people from all over the world came here to help in that venture and win a place for themselves. It was impossible at that time to foresee that these United States, of all nations, should fall into the same insensible pattern as the old countries from whence the immigrants hailed; that employment should become a privilege, granted by a few, and that hundreds, later thousands, then millions should be doomed to months or years or sometimes whole life-spans of inactivity, crippling their muscles, brains and self-confidence, a fate worse than death; that the nation as a whole should suffer the loss of billions of man-hours, sorely needed to keep it in shape, in adequate supply of energy, food, clean and healthful air and water, and to keep its money supply stable and sufficient for carrying out required functions. If our Founding Fathers had been able to foresee this incredible trend, they would have included continuous full employment as every citizen's inalienable right, and as a requirement for the health and vigor of the nation - all embedded in the Constitution.

Some, at least, of our economists, businessmen and Congressmen have understood this and are fighting for this most important of all measures: continuous full employment. This could be achieved in a number of viable ways, all with great advantage to our economy, our life patterns, our freedoms, our international relations. The difficulty is luring the twentieth-century distressed and despairing minds into action. It is not necessary for the citizen-voter to understand in detail how it can be done. All she or he has to do is distinguish between the clear-minded and the befuddled, and send the former to Congress or the White House or to head any type of required action.

Forced unemployment, even for one single man for one year, is never "required for the good of the economy". It means an intolerable loss to the economy. It is also the principal cause of inflation. Money paid to people who don't produce is basically inflationary. Though a rich nation can afford some such payments, they become necessary only when an ignorant or corrupt leadership permits the nation to lapse into severe unemployment.

There is a world out there, millions hungry, other millions freezing, and eight million "rich" Americans sitting idly before our television sets, worrying where the groceries will be coming from tomorrow; and about the thousands of tasks that must be done but aren't done here at home: more careful farming to preserve and develop the priceless soil, so it may yield good food rather than overgrown, energy-wasting, chemically loaded questionables; pollution-free energy sources, such as from ocean thermal differences, the sun, wind, geothermal.

I brought the French research results on the Ocean Thermal Difference system to this country in 1947 and after years of continued research here, we were ready for full-blown plants in the fifties, but we had to wait for the stunning blow of quadrupling oil prices before the National Science Foundation became serious, in the seventies. Now, finally, decisive reports have come from grantees all over the nation. On behalf of the University of Massachusetts, a principal investigator, Professor William E. Heronemus, writes in his 1975 spring report:

> "Any competent man with a broad-gauge industrial sense of what can be achieved by 1975 US industry using materials, energy and financial base, available for the next 3 decades, will agree that OTECS (Ocean Thermal Difference Energy Conversion Systems) is that which could be done best. The results of this study can be summarized as follows:
>
> a. Enough has been done now by many to guarantee that OTECS is technically feasible.
>
> b. There are clear-cut pathways to make OTECS economically preferable, not just feasible or competitive.
>
> c. Large-scale development, acquisition and deployment of

OTECS would be almost identical to the World War II ship-building effort. The World has never seen another industrial effort so easy to get started and so capable of producing prodigious numbers of high-class products. (Underlined in the original report) This economy could flood the world with OTECS if there were simply a desire to do so, and the effort would spread from the waterfront back into every portion of the industrialized hinterland like the wildfire of prosperity, if we so desire. The OTECS program which follows is a summary of what could and should be done. Supporting detail can be found in the numerous technical reports and progress reports produced to date by J. Hilbert Anderson, the University of Massachusetts team, the Carnegie Mellon University team, the TRW-Global Marine-United Constructors & Engineers team and the Lockheed-Bechtel team. . ."

At this date numerous more reports from universities and industries all over the nation are out. Following is a brief excerpt of the *Lockheed-Bechtel Report*, summer 1975:

"This report has established that the use of ocean thermal power is technologically feasible at an acceptable investment cost and at an operating cost comparable to other existing and proposed plants. Half the earth's surface in the tropic zone consists of ocean suitable for OTEC operation. The basic energy source - the sun - will continue whether man makes use of it or not. The environmental consequences are believed to be almost wholly benign for any foreseeable level of exploitation. The implementation of the demonstration OTEC plant and the subsequent authorization for a chain of production plants would be a major contribution to solving the energy crisis and should become an urgent national priority for the U.S."

The "Fourth Workshop" of this Ocean Thermal Difference Energy Conversion System, held in New Orleans 22 - 24 March 1977, featured four hundred dedicated scientists and engineers from the cream of U. S. industry and universities, as compared with one hundred thirty active participants (out of an audience of five hundred attending) at the previous workshop in Houston, Texas in May, 1975. The mood had changed from piece-meal research to demands for building several plants for various purposes simultaneously. An example was *The Parallel-Telescopic Development Program for Ocean Thermal Energy Conversion*, proposed by Dr. David F. Mayer of the University of New Orleans. This bold yet cautious plan calls for immediate overall design of six configurations, then building of the three designs considered best, all in the course of four years. By 1981 practical power plants would be available and by 1980 "hundreds of them could be producing power, hydrogen, ammonia, substituting natural gas, alcohol and gasoline. The total estimated cost, half a billion dollars over four years, is less than the cost of one week's imported oil."

> "The basic concept," writes Dr. Mayer, "is that work be done concurrently rather than serially. Also, when an overall plant design is undertaken, the engineers immediately address the essential questions which must be answered to design the plant. Otherwise, as in the present case, there is a great deal of disoriented research on relatively insignificant problems which have little bearing upon the actual plant design process."

Dr. Mayer's proposal frees us from our confusing '70's, recalling our enterprising '40's.

On April 21, 1977, Professor William E. Heronemus summarized our energy policy in a *Chancellor's Lecture Series* talk at the University of Massachusetts at Amherst. He further proposed building large Ocean Thermal Energy Conversion plants abroad and in the U.S., along with wind mills in appropriate locations, at a yearly cost starting with two billion dollars in 1978 and increasing over the years. To start the ball rolling, he took leave from the university, joined the firm Alfa-Laval that has a unique record in such OTEC components as heat exchangers, pumping, pipelines, etc. His own and this company's other employees' estimates envisage such energy systems will cost no more than our current ones, with no pollution, no fuel shortages, no price increases, and a simple, labor- intensive technology offering more ample and more balanced employment.

The fifth OTEC workshop in Miami Beach in 1978 and further developments show promise of achievement and also indications of further delay. Our peculiar power structure and thought patterns have delayed OTEC for decades, and may eventually stop further development - of this as well as other benign systems. When well-known technologies become fashionable, as the century-old OTEC did in the seventies, government as well as scientific bodies feel obliged to make an "evaluation". For this purpose, they choose scientists who never worked with OTEC and know nothing about it. Being presented with 100 pounds of literature, they jump happily into the same traps in which the pioneers found themselves decades ago. The only people able to judge are the "OTECERS" who worked for years on this matter. But these are shunned as "advocates" ready to subvert, deceive and seduce the naive public. This weird superstition is nurtured by the civil service system and the government structure. When a civil servant works with and appreciates OTEC for some years, he is replaced by a newcomer who has to repeat all the old mistakes again and so delays or stops the project.

The 1940s, during which we fought and won World War II, was also a most productive decade in economic discussion and understanding. Yale's Dr. John H.G. Pierson, of United Nations fame, Harvard's Dr. John Philip Wernette, now at Ann Arbor, and Dr. Leon Keyserling, the enlightened Chairman of the Council of Economic Advisors to President Truman, all began their penetrating research and publications in this decade and were actually listened to then. Today, when we need their insight and advice more than ever, they are virtually unknown, even though they continue their inputs to press and TV sharper than ever. Today, instead, people listen awed to slogans such as "Get the government out of the Market Place!" (or further into it), as if anybody can ever get out of or into the market place. We are in it, forever, governments and individuals. Those who cry the loudest are connected with giant enterprises which live and breathe by the grace of government interference and special protection of their interests. It is the small and daring enterprises breaking new ground that still work on the principle of free enterprise. To them the Government is a constant threat, a merciless agent for the giants who wallow in out-dated methods and equipment, and want to kill competitors. In this senseless fight, the workers suffer, eight million of them at present.

Before quoting from relevant books and articles, may we have a look at present reactions from Washington, DC?

Being fond of Chairmen of the Council of Economic Advisors to Presidents from Leon Keyserling's time, I wrote to the present incumbent, Dr. Alan Greenspan, per 1 October 1974.

> "An admirer of your integrity and ingenuity, I noticed a news release, 29 September, quoting you, 'No one has offered a solution toward improving the inflation and employment situation.' It may have been a misquote. Nevertheless, I enclose my August 28 letter to the Vice President in which I list four economists having offered such solution. I listed these four because I know their views and working methods. There are many more, of course, of varying political views, which is an asset in our present critical situation.
>
> "In the United States, private enterprise has already solved the major employment and stability requirements. Only a small additional effort is needed for an adequate solution. Harvard's Dr. John Philip Wernette (now with Ann Arbor) proposes to create a 'stabilization board' to supply this additional service. He first explained it in his book *Financing Full Employment* (Harvard University Press, 1945). Yale's Dr. John H.G. Pierson (now at 101 Lewis Street, Greenwich, Conn. 06830) wants Congress to do the job, in the spirit of the 1946 Employment Act. He now proposes that Congress shall guarantee full employment and other specified economic conditions required to attain this along with adequate stability. This is achieved by trial and error in our country because of the unique resilience of our economy, as realized also by such foreign observers as Sir William Beveridge and A. de V. Leigh, for 35 years Secretary General of the London Chamber of Commerce, a driving force be-

hind trade at his time, a close friend of Herbert Feis of the State Department and myself. Congressman Reuss and Senators Henry Jackson and Hubert Humphrey well know and appreciate Pierson's views. Pierson's book of 1964 most clearly explains his views though his first book about this was in 1941. The last was in 1972. His articles have graced the New York Times and professional economic journals until this day.

"Full employment has recently been temporarily realized in West Germany, France, and Norway, though without money stability and more by accident than design. It remains for the more comprehensive and independent American economy to make full employment, along with a relatively stable price level. a permanent reality. Some members of the Kennedy Administration worked with me on multi-surveys that would show our real potentials - preliminary to full employment under stable conditions, though not a required preliminary. This revealed to us the vast untapped resources in our nation and what we may achieve if we wish.

"May I suggest you fortify your council with Dr. John H.G. Pierson or Dr. Wernette or both?"

The letter to Vice President Rockefeller of 28 August, 1974, referred to in the above letter, ran as follows:

"It is a privilege to address the most experienced person in the present Administration and possibly in the nation as a whole - on the matter of the nation's economy.

"It has been heartening to watch the steps already initiated. However, most of the gentlemen consulted appear to view employment and inflation as alternatives. They seem to believe we must curb employment to fight inflation. This crude, simplistic and totally erroneous theory should be balanced against more wide-ranging views represented by such economists as Harvard's John Philip Wernette, the University of California's Seymour Harris (Senior Advisor to the Treasury under two previous administrations), Leon Keyserling, Chairman of the

President's Council of Economic Advisors to a previous administration, and others.

"The clearest, most conservative, most cautious and most experienced representative of this group is Yale's Dr. John H.G. Pierson, 101 Lewis Street, Greenwich, Conn. 06830, who, through leading positions in business, in the US Government and in the United Nations, has sharpened and improved the views he acquired and held from his early years. A quick grasp of his views may be obtained by reading first the summation in the enclosed issue of the Congressional Record of the expected results of his full employment policy. The rest of the article explains this policy's conditions and functions.* His four books provide more details.

"I feel that a consulting body not including Dr. Pierson or his views would be a tragedy for the nation. And who am I, who dare make such a statement? I have worked in almost all imaginable capacities in 65 countries throughout all parts of the world. To some I am known as the restorer of Norway's economy after the Nazi occupiers had smashed it. To others I am blamed as the originator of the abortive plan to kidnap Hitler and shorten World War II by eight months. It was abortive because Franklin Roosevelt turned it down, 'We must beat the Germans so they know it.' I headed a UN mission to Tunisia, hoping to bring the economy of the Southern part into shape. I worked with a previous administration on multi-surveys we hoped would initiate inflation-free full employment. All the while I have delved into humbler work, for a living, at the same time maintaining and increasing my knowledge of the details that form the building blocks of nations' lives and economies. And from 1938 I have watched and admired the spotless, impressive, incomparable career of the man who has now graced the United States by accepting the Vice-Presidency.

The Vice-President gracefully answered, "Thank you for your recent message and enclosure. I appreciate your taking the time to share your views on the nation's economy with me."

The Chairman of the Council of Economic Advisors, through his special assistant, went into more detail. "Thank you for your letter to Alan Greenspan and for bringing the work of Mr. Pierson and Mr. Wernette to our attention. Mr. Greenspan stated that, unfortunately, 'no one had offered a solution' which would effect an immediate and simultaneous solution in inflation, production, employment and interest rates. The period immediately ahead will be difficult, in that progress cannot be made on all fronts simultaneously, and realism dictates that we recognize this and choose which of the unpleasant consequences we face has the highest priority. Otherwise we are not likely to make progress either with inflation or with production or unemployment. Once the reduction in inflation is underway the proposals of Mr. Pierson and Mr. Wernette may be more applicable."

My response to this message, and further correspondence with a Chairman of the Council of Economic Advisors to an earlier president, with senators and newsmen and selected economists, will follow as illustrations to coming chapters.

* This article is presented as an appendix at the end of this book.

CHILDREN'S HOUR

All who might help lift our economy to a higher and more natural level were once children. What happened to them then? How did that affect their later behavior, judgment, and ability to listen, think and feel?

Yale University was the first to build a dome, of such wonder that a child placed inside could be watched by note-taking scholars outside; the child did not see these watchers, and could not even see the dome. So, he behaved without the disturbance of outside influence.

Computers now on the drawing board will tell more about children's' reactions, but we don't have to wait for them. Sensitive individuals of all faiths have for thousands of years sneaked their consciousness inside other beings, including children, and monitored their thoughts and feelings partly by ignoring their own. Mothers have been the greatest of such sensitives, or mystics, without even knowing these words.

So, we have a solid base of knowledge about the child and its mind. First of all, we know that each one is different, unique. After this admission, we may list what appear to be "general trends".

Our scientific community loves to ask questions of grown-ups and children and arrange the answers in graphs and matrixes. Foundations love to grant funds for such research. Mothers who delve into their children's minds, and some yogis and Sufis who can memorize and relive their entire lives from earliest childhood, look with some distaste at these simplistic and oblique statistics, the kind of questions asked, and the acceptance of the answers they receive as valid responses. Why do not these investigators supplement their statistics with a bit of warm, living memory of their own? Anybody can recall at least some of their past if they try.

Children are supposed to be so awfully happy, but I recall my own childhood as the hardest and most frightening time of my life though I had the best possible parents and always enough to eat. But my parents' problems weighed heavier on me than on them. My father's constant fight against a hierarchy that placed an Army man as head of hydrographic work made me forever distrust hierarchies. Their influence, I thought, was insincere, deadening.

What do children of unemployed workers feel and think? What kind of mind and heart are built into them? Can anyone blame them if they determine to wage war on a community that treats its members that way? Oh, I know all about foreign conspiracies. I have lived and worked in Russia, East and West Germany, China and Japan. I know of the schemes to destroy America. These would have no effect whatever if we kept our own house in order. Actually, we should treasure the schemes directed against us. They are necessary awakeners. Without them we would decay and rot. To be surprised at the increase in crime and sabotage, when we keep eight million unemployed, is a worse hypocrisy than I thought my countrymen capable.

I sent an earlier version of this book to Dr. Jule Eisenbud, former Professor of Psychiatry at Columbia. Dr. Eisenbud is not just a psychiatrist, but an awake psychiatrist. He replied,

"I read your book with much enjoyment. Too bad there aren't more of your kind in Washington, D.C., although I can well understand why there are not."

Later I sent him some similar chapters from an other book, on the environment. To that he replied,

"I had great pleasure and admiration reading your truly farsighted and humanistic chapters. I would like to look forward to being able to do the type of freewheeling thinking you do when I am at your age, but I sometimes wonder if I have sufficiently escaped the gravitational pull of my built-in (or rather educated-in - programmed) aberrations (as you have it). Perhaps, if I could once have the type of out-of-the-body experience you describe having had, I could continue to keep my thinking fresh and creative. Perhaps we should all periodically 'stop the world' as Castaneda put it.

"Anyway, I admire your continued interest in 'teaching the world'. Long may you keep at it. With all good wishes of all seasons."

Returning now to the reply to my plea for full employment by the Chairman of the Council for Economic Advisors through his Assistant, John Davis, quoted on the last page of the previous chapter, my reply to Mr. Davis was:

> "Your good letter of October 9 was very much appreciated. I sent a copy to Dr. John H.G. Pierson, hoping he might reply. Instead, he gave a talk to the people in Greenwich, Connecticut, 'Full Employment as a Means of Combating Inflation'. The point is, his or Wernette's plans are not something to apply after inflation has been licked, but a means to combat it, and possibly one of the most necessary means. Observing the market place, the nation as a whole, isn't it pretty clear that unemployment is a contributing cause for inflation? And we cannot have either full employment or stable prices except through a guarantee, by such a body as Congress, for example. It is well within the economic power of the United States to guarantee an adequate level of consumer spending along with virtually full employment.
>
> "I really have no doubt that the able economists on the Council of Economic Advisors know this, but have reservations about recommending politically precarious solutions. But proposing a professionally correct solution may serve your party, as well as the nation, better than submitting to an obsolete political climate.
>
> "This letter is written to you and also to Dr. Greenspan, to whom I trust you will show it."

Naturally, there was no further response. With my penchant for Chairmen of Councils of Economic Advisors, I sent an earlier version of this book to Dr. Leon Keyserling, President Truman's Council of Economic Advisors' Chairman. Dr. Keyserling responded,

"I appreciated very much the letter and materials you sent me on December 31, 1972, and am returning the materials herewith. I would have replied sooner, but for many distractions.

"Needless to say, I am entirely in accord with your general thesis and its development. Keep up the good work.

"I have a few reservations, which I can state only very succinctly. In my view, you give too much credit to Samuelson and Burns. Burns is now obsessed about holding down expenditures and about as worried as to where the money is coming from as anyone could be. Samuelson is much better, but even he is expressive of very much of the conventional viewpoint. One of the biggest difficulties, to which little attention is being paid, is the outmoded views of the great preponderance of well-known and other economists. I do not believe that there is any solution to monetary control along appropriate lines, short of much greater responsibility of the Federal Reserve System to the President and the Congress. There is no more reason why it should be entirely independent as a practical matter than why tax policy or price-wage policy, when we have it, should be independent of public control. I do not share the view that the *Employment Act* was a weak statute. Its very virtue was that it conveyed plenary authority without limitation, and the trouble is that the responsibility has not been assumed. You are much too favorable to the Kennedy years. Its policies were inadequate and its central policy, in the form of massive tax cuts for the wrong people (enacted under Johnson), was wrong and damaging for a variety of reasons which I have repeatedly set forth. I do not agree that full employment produces more inflation, and I am enclosing a copy of my 1971 pamphlet which covers this subject and also covers many of the other matters in which we are mutually interested. While there were frustrations and shortcomings while I was Chairman of the CEA, I think your treatment is too negative. Actually, we made a better average record on employment, growth and price stability than any administration since, and I reviewed this in articles in the *New Republic* on October 3 and October 24, 1970. I am surprised that you credit Galbraith with a way toward full employment. In *The Affluent Society* his basic thesis was that we should surrender our national commitment to full employment, on the spurious ground that this was necessary to avoid inflation. His pronouncements since then have moved in both directions.

"Thanks for the opportunity to comment, and I look forward to hearing from you again. With all good wishes..."

When I read and re-read this deeply satisfying response from a former Chairman of the Council of Economic Advisors to a President, I feel like repeating what Dr. Jule Eisenbud, Professor of Psychiatry at Columbia, wrote me, "Too bad there aren't more people like you in Washington, D.C."

In the above letter Dr. Keyserling refers to 'Samuelson'. This is Dr. Paul A. Samuelson, the Nobel Prize winning economics professor at the Massachusetts Institute of Technology. I had an interesting response from Dr. Samuelson to my own letter to him of 26 November 1970:

"The author of *Chapter 19: Fiscal Policy and Full Employment Without Inflation ('Economics: An Introductory Analysis')* received a letter May 4, 1966. John H.G. Pierson offered in that letter the fusion of two able minds and so influential, together, that they could have saved the United States from dropping into a secondary role and leaving the world confused, without alternatives.

"I am trying to figure out why you did not answer. Did you feel Congress was not yet able, at that time, to understand that there was an economic basis for guaranteeing insured full employment and a level of consumer spending? Or were you even in doubt that such a basis existed at that time? But you could not doubt that it exists now, today? And there is no doubt that several Congressmen understand this and would sponsor such a bill if so advised by a panel of well- established economists? Whether such a bill would be passed by Congress is another matter, about which we have no responsibility. Nothing has ever been achieved without a willingness to try, against odds.

"This is written, not to try to involve you in any activity or publicity, at least not at this time, only to point out the great similarity between your above chapter and Dr. Pierson's plans, or for that matter, the related full employment plans of Dr. John Philip Wernette, the Harvard man who went to Ann Arbor, and Dr. Leon Keyserling, Chairman of the Council of Economic Advisors to President Truman. Melville Ulmer's articles in the *New Republic* could be included.

"As you know, our scientific developments in vital areas have practically been stopped. We are already far behind, and our friends in other countries are bewildered and sad. We can still regain our lost lead, but we may not have more than 2-3 years grace, so any awakening must begin now, ten minutes ago and not three seconds late. We are now, today, technically and economically able to lift ourselves to a level where our ecology, our feeding, our ocean resources and defense needs may be satisfactorily solved. Urban developments would follow. Only economic superstition and a few worse sentiments are temporarily stopping us.

"Who am I? Unlike John Maynard Keynes, I realized before starting college that economics, as taught, was irrelevant so I majored in engineering (which I found also rather irrelevant). I made a 1. (best available) in economics by answering questions tongue-in-cheek (as I knew they wanted the answers). Through the years I have read and experienced more economics than most. I helped the 'Young Turks'; the Norwegians (in remaking a wrecked economy after World War II). I went to Tunisia on behalf of the United Nations and wasted the time of important J. F. Kennedy administration officials.

"Your 1951 book is better than anything offered today in College or University economics courses."

Dr. Samuelson answered, per 1 December 1970: "I have no wish to criticize Pierson's view. But I am not prepared to make them mine."

A beautiful sensitivity is shown in this answer, by a superb teacher in a democratic country. However, when one considers the striking similarity of the two views, one would have hoped that fruitful public discussion would have ensued, resulting possibly in action, rather than delicate neutrality and no action.

A young college student pointed out to me this similarity.

THE UNSETTLED

In their senior year of high school they came to me. They had found out what nobody else had found out: That I was working on the challenging riddles of energy, ecology, the economy. I had sent book manuscripts and articles east and west. They came back. Nobody cared. To these young people I sent nothing, said nothing. But they knew. They pressed their teacher to have me talk to their class. They did not swallow blindly my ideas. They asked polite but sharp questions. Then they asked me to join a study group they had formed, that met after school. We were accommodated in the spacious home of one of the youngsters. His parents thanked me for my interest in the youngsters (it was I who should have thanked the youngsters for their interest in me). They wondered why their youngsters seemed to feel closer to me than to themselves. It comforted them to hear that I had the same trouble with my own children and it was not through them I had reached these other youngsters. The parent-child relationship may seem perfect when the child needs and craves authority and guidance. But this early relationship becomes an almost insurmountable obstacle when the youngster strikes out on his own. Then he no longer needs direct guidance, nor does he remember that he did need it before. He just sees in his parents an intolerably repressive force. Even if the parent tries to abandon all authority, he is not believed, or accepted. An almost superhuman effort is required to tide the relationship over from the time of authority to the time of freedom. Both parties must have a will to understand and rebuild the bridge.

Do these youngsters fit the term "unsettled"? As much as I do. We are unsettled until we have made it possible for anyone to sail right into a fully paid job the minute he wants to and thus contribute to the urgent rebuilding of our society. Are these youngsters liable to drop into the bomb-throwing crowd? Less likely than any of us, for they enjoy the rare gift of confidence, confidence in themselves and in our nation, confidence that they can build a viable society. They would never do anything that could jeopardize this work. Only the weaklings, who know or feel they cannot achieve, will turn to guns and bombs, egged on by Communists, conservatives or law and order guardians, native or foreign, on whose shoulders they weep and sigh. Their attitude may have been triggered by well-meant but traumatic parent-child relationships. Court procedures, prosecutors, defense lawyers, judges and jailings can only add to the destruction. The only ones who might reach them and remake them are the kind of youngsters who remade me.

One day, one of my young friends came along with a book. "I thought this was something in your line," he said. The author was John H.G. Pierson, an economist who had recently retired from the position of Science and Economics Advisor to the Secretary General of the United Nations, and who from 1941 had worked for guaranteed full employment. I am ashamed to say I had never heard of him. The book, *Insuring Full Employment,* had been published in 1964. It was electrifying. I immediately got in touch with the author, this fall in 1968. Here was a man who had constantly been in the news, who had authored the most sophisticated of the statements ascribed to and uttered by a succession of Secretary Generals of the United Nations, and whose first book *Full Employment* (Yale University Press, 1941) was hailed by Yale's President to be "not merely the book of the year but of the coming decade". Yet, he accepted and treated this humble unknown as a brother, even an older one. He has the kind of heart that sees the need for useful employment for every willing hand; he has the kind of mind who sees the enormous benefits of such a policy upon the national and the international scene.

When I sent an earlier and clumsier version of this book to an Eastern publisher, Dr. Pierson took a chance on his distinguished reputation by addressing that publisher as follows:

"I understand that you may be considering publishing Mr. Bryn Beorse's book, *Every Willing Hand*. Having read the manuscript with fascination, I venture to write to say that I hope you do decide to publish it.

"This espousal by me may appear suspect in view of the favorable notice which my work on full employment receives in Mr. Beorse's closing pages. Please believe, though, that my main reasons for hoping to see this book in print are impersonal ones. One is my conviction that Mr. Beorse renders an important public service by stressing as he does how much our success, or lack of it, in providing jobs for all who want them will really matter, i.e. how profoundly it will affect our ability as a nation to weather these tough times by facing up to fundamental human and material problems. But my chief reason is not economic at all-rather it is the extraordinary effect that this wide-ranging, philosophical essay has produced on me as a general reader. And will, I believe, equally produce on other readers who have the opportunity to view it whole.

"One doesn't have to agree with all of Mr. Beorse's opinions - I don't, with all - to realize that this is both a wise and a beautiful book. America was lucky to get a man like that away from the Norwegians. As for those essential sales - the JFK link should help; the somewhat disorganized presentation can surely do no harm in this day and age; and at least our youth, I feel sure, will really like what he says. In short, though all such books are doubtless a business gamble, the odds this time would seem to me to be favorable."

Two years later, when he heard I was seeking a new job, without any request from my side, he sent me the following:

"There are many people who cannot see the forest for the trees, but you, happily, are not among them. During the several years in which it has been my privilege to come to know you rather well, I have been enormously impressed with the wide range of your experience and the acuteness of your per-

ceptions - as so strikingly evidenced in your varied writings-
yet perhaps even more impressive is your capacity for overview
and perspective. Especially gratifying to me, in view of my own
long-time identification with the cause of full employment,
is your deep appreciation of how critically important for the
whole future of America, at home and also in our foreign relations, the question of the policies that will guarantee everybody
a chance to work has now, in fact, become."

I am embarrassed to report further on this unusual relationship
which, after these four years of boom, ought to have dropped into
a deep recession by all good prescriptions. After three more years,
however, a 1975 letter from one to the other began,

"You are a man in a million - actually a billion would be closer to
the truth. . ."

Such a relationship, of course, disqualifies any one of the two to
comment validly on the other or his views, according to accepted
worldly wisdom. The non-worldly wisdom, embodied in philosophy or religion, holds the opposite view: that without close and in-
tense sympathy you cannot understand or evaluate another. American management concepts have tried generously to embrace both.
You learn in modern managerial courses that supervisors must show
sympathy. If they cannot feel it, they must at least pretend. They
must ask about the employee's family, his health, his problems. And
try to show interest in the answers.

Some who tried to practice what they thus learned often found it
wasn't boring at all, but painfully challenging. They became amazed,
shaken and deeply involved, so deeply that they forgot to put on the
right tie clasp the next morning.

There is a third way, beyond either sympathy or emotional neutrality. In Paris, France, Pierre Duclos was picked up by a suave,
handsome Parisian gendarme after having slugged a victim with a
bicycle chain. The gendarme, his emotions under control, did not
slug Pierre but politely asked,

"Jail or Doctor?"

"Doctor? What does that mean?"

"Some kind of treatment. Painless. If it works you will be out in a few weeks; free. If it doesn't work you will go to jail."

"Hum, what can I lose?"

So Pierre was sent to the S.E.C.M.A. clinics where Dr. Jacques Ménétrier's catalyzer treatment was applied. The contents of a small vial was poured into his mouth. He was told not to swallow but keep the contents in the mouth until notified. It tasted like water. Pierre did not know that a tiny amount of metal was in that water - gold, silver, copper or some combination, according to the preceding diagnosis.

Pierre took great care to follow instructions and even appear impressed, for the hospital was better than the jail; why, here were even nurses, and some of them were cute. He wasn't going to spoil a good thing by showing anybody how utterly stupid he thought this whole business was.

The treatment was repeated several times a day. After two weeks doctors began asking him questions. Why, what was the matter with him? Pierre found to his disgust that he answered entirely differently from what he would have done before. Had these damned doctors made him a sissy?

Not really that either. He seemed to delve deeper into things, understand more. What in blazes had happened to him?

After three weeks Pierre was released. The doctors felt he would hardly hit anyone with a bicycle chain again. He was told to come back in a month. He did. He had come to like the place and the nurses. Besides, he hated to think what might happen to him if he disobeyed. They tested him at the clinic. There was no indication of any backslide. He was given another dose and told to be back in three months. He looked at the nurse and hoped it could have been sooner.

Doctors in Germany, England, America looked on fascinated as delinquency by and by disappeared in Paris. They sent letters of praise and even gold medals to Dr. Ménétrier, the inventor and founder. Not for one moment did it occur to any of them to try out the method in his own country.

Through my fluttering mind monitored by that Yogi-simulator, the other part of me, I have portrayed what I believe to be the top and the bottom of the social ladder of the young. Now I am coming to some who have heard and been impressed by that ancient bugle. That should place them on the straight path, shouldn't it?

By a first glance it would seem so. They have accepted the Episcopalian or the Presbyterian or Unitarian or Catholic faith and church. On paper they have accepted. As a teenager and a monitor of teenagers, I am close enough to look a little deeper. Their minds are not where their words are: their words to parents, teachers, preachers and even friends. Secretly they ask questions: What does this word "Episcopalian" mean? Or "Lutheran"? Or "Catholic"? What connection do these words have with that prophet in the deserts of Palestine? These words did not even exist at that time.

What about the word Christian? Even that wasn't much used at the time, certainly not by that impressive prophet. What have we contrived from his simple, touching words flung out two thousand years ago? Earnest ministers and priests join in asking such questions but not-so-well-informed congregations and bland church-policy makers push them back in line.

The ancient bugle could still have the greatest influence in our cybernetic age, if it were played in the style and spirit in which it first sounded.

"Civilization" has been blamed for having changed and corrupted the ancient bugle. Only certain aspects of civilization have had that effect and not, for example, the technological or cybernetic part of civilization.

Modern religions and the sciences of history, behaviorism and biology see Catholics and Protestants, Christians and Buddhists, theists and atheists, hawks and doves, liberals and conservatives. Mathematics, physics and cybernetics are not concerned with such distinctions and do not judge or categorize clients but serve all equally, with equanimity, like he who said, "I have not come to give a new law but to confirm the Law." And, "In my Father's House there are many mansions." (He didn't say that some of these mansions were false and that their inhabitants would go to hell.)

When people called him complicated names and praised him, he responded, "Call me not good; only one is good - God," in the same vein as a computer or a computer-operator would say, "Neither the computer nor its operator is good but we try to find TRUTH and truth only is good."

While some grown-ups wring their hands over youngsters who do not blindly accept their views, we youngsters wring our hands over grown-ups who live by belief instead of truth and try to drive us into the same trap.

Our cybernetic age seeks truth only. Not that we have it but we seek it, like the artist who tries to paint the perfect picture. He does not succeed entirely, but he comes closer. In trying to paint this perfect picture, we are willing to listen to tales, any and all, but don't try to ram them down our throats or you'll offend the God in us!

Many a preacher soars high above his imposed faith but is afraid to admit his thoughts. Why then does he expect us youngsters to hear and respect? His creed still seems burdened with the lead of past superstition.

Grown-ups have another clear and concise duty to us youngsters; to provide us with an outlet for our energy and drive, and offer full employment to anyone who wants to work so he may eat, feel needed, marry and have children, channel his talents and urges into legal outlets the moment he is ready!

Why, the grown-ups haven't been able to do this among themselves yet! Why, then, do they try to talk and preach themselves out of their obvious responsibility? Do they not heed the onrushing flood of thundering young humanity?

The task of securing well-paid jobs for every willing worker is not superhuman, not in the U.S.A. Thousands of citizens stand ready to work out full employment the minute they are so authorized; among them practically all economists, according to one such economist now in a central position with our government. But our society is not yet run by economists, nor by other knowledgeable people; for example, those who worked abroad with thousands without first asking what education they had or if they could read or write.

The U.S.A. may be the only nation now ready for full employment (which, incidentally, would increase, not diminish our economic power), but the political body has not yet realized it. The old frontier that offered an outlet for ambitious youth still exists, but is latent inside our social order. It requires united effort to put it into operation. No single youth or oldster can do that alone.

When we act, and when everyone earns enough to marry when love beckons and sex roars, then the world will make sense even to us youngsters who, relaxed, may begin to wonder about life - and LIFE. If we want a friend and companion on this path of wondering, we might join Admiral Richard F. Byrd who was staying alone for many weeks in the Antarctic wastelands. He developed an eerie feeling that he was not alone. He grabbed paper and pencil and began to write. Soon he had a complete conversation going with this unseen, unknown friend.

Was he "hearing voices"? An officer and scientist had nothing to gain, much to lose by publishing these observations. A sober reader may agree that he remained sane and very accurate through the ordeal. His observations have been shared by a great many people in all walks of life, in crowds, in jungles, in Arctic or Antarctic wastelands. They experience an "it," common to all religions "and," concludes Admiral Byrd, "a good English word is GOD."

GENERATION BRIDGE

Why do Chinese and Japanese families maintain the precarious parent-child relationship more successfully than the rest of us? Are they more tolerant of their children, or are the latter more respectful of their parents?

When I lived in the home of an American Colonel stationed in Japan, his Japanese servants practically ran the house, decided on menus, cleaning arrangements, even on what the Colonel and his wife should wear each day. It was a beautiful and efficient game, finally resulting in the Colonel paying the man servant's way through medical school in the United States, and other well-deserved benefits accruing to the girl servants. This supposedly precarious relationship between two basically different cultures and resulting from a devastating war, turned out better and healthier than many of our most well-established domestic family relationships.

Un-bridged generation gaps or, for that matter, gaps of any serious nature between either age groups or other groups in a society or nation disturb and confuse the purpose and intent of such a society and makes sensible policies difficult or impossible to carry out. The gaps themselves and how to deal with them demand all the attention and energy of the decision-makers. All other plans and policies are left waiting, such as work priorities, and following those, employment opportunities so that, for example, gap-ridden societies drift into major unemployment. Recognize a case illustrating this, anyone?

When a Japanese executive reaches retirement age, he is retained; regularly, as a consultant; in particular, responsible for the proper training of younger executives. There is no generation gap, only a well-trafficked generation bridge. When an American executive reaches retirement age, battle stations are manned, the warring factions mobilizing all their skills demanding either the executive's final retirement or, the other side, claiming he's an exception and should be permitted to continue working for the good of the company. There is no free competition any longer, just a socially enforced handicap. Let someone calculate how much energy is spent, how many urgent decisions are postponed while debilitating fighting is going on.

Should we praise ourselves for being more fiercely independent and less respectful, thus serving efficiency? Are we serving efficiency that way?

The child, during his first years, is enjoying the parents' firm guidance. The parents, in turn, enjoy being guides. In due time the child craves independence, more and more. Even if the parents comply, the memory of earlier firm guidance irritates the child at this period, if not a Chinese or Japanese child, and the greatest wisdom is required to rebuild a bridge that is falling apart. Every person develops certain concepts or thought patterns that become sacred, especial to the young. A parent must abandon any wish to impose his own concepts or thoughts, however apparently justified, be it in science, religion, morality or just social amenities. But this is not enough - the attitude of the wise parent must be one of respectful silence, waiting for the youngster to talk rather than clamoring for attention to present one's own indomitable concepts.

The entire human race may be too fond of concepts and theories today. Ancient Yogis and Sufis and modern minds of similar trends de-emphasize thought structures or ignore them. This may be a good idea to try for all of us, though some philosophers would have hysterics. Their science, lately, has deteriorated into a listing of concepts, mistaking this for schools of philosophy. Are the easier generation relationships in China and Japan due to less concept-ridden thought patterns in those countries?

But there must be something sacred inviolate that everybody must accept. There is, though not in the shape of words or concepts. Life is sacred, living beings are. The concepts of these living beings are not sacred and need not be shared, but should be respected.

When her only son turned out a yogi, at an early age, my mother of a lineage of Lutheran clergy, didn't bat an eye. She showed deep and touching respect for my views as well as for my new yoga friends. When, at 27, I became a Sufi she was equally respectful. When I, a yogi and Sufi, saw my only son turn into a fundamentalist Christian, his minister boasting to me that he "would never return to that Sufi nonsense," I kept my cool and my respect. Besides, I guessed what would happen; my son turned quietly away from the fundamentalists, and began questioning me guardedly about yoga and meditation.

An older man made inquiries about yoga and meditation at that same time, and for more compelling reasons. Dr. Carl Simonton had been involved in cancer research since 1966. In the following, the doctor's own explanations are exclusively used to avoid inaccuracies, and because they represent the yogic view better than most yoga exponents do. There are also unusual and useful generation bridges involved.

Dr. Simonton began work with high hopes. After three years he was disappointed. He sensed a need for free and fresh thinking in this area, but with the tremendous responsibility of human life involved he dared not think, far less act, outside current concepts and teachings. Then he heard a talk by a prominent immunotherapist who held that every one had cancer many times during his or her life time and that clinical cancer only developed for one of two reasons: First, that particularly resistant cancer cells developed, or that particularly strong cancer cells invaded the body; second, that the body's "immune mechanism" or host resistance broke down to some degree and allowed these abnormal cells to grow into a size which was detectable. This basic host mechanism is the same that destroys all abnormal cells presented to the body bacteria, viruses and the like.

The speaker had tested his theory on terminal leukemic patients who had failed on all other forms of chemotherapy. He had made a solution of concentrate of their abnormal white cells and applied this solution to a prepared area of the skin in the hope of evoking an immune response that would in turn attack disease in the body. He achieved a fifty percent remission rate in these leukemic patients. Then other doctors became interested and tried the same method. They obtained only half as good results, or less. Following the latter's only moderate success, many more tried, and the results became less and less encouraging.

It was this apparent "law of diminishing return" that particularly interested Dr. Simonton. Obviously, the inventor's drive and enthusiasm, born of hard work and resulting conviction, had inspired both himself and his patients. If he could emulate this enthusiasm, this drive, thought Dr. Simonton, he could do as well as the originator. This was, he decided, first and foremost a matter of the mind. This discovery made Dr. Simonton, in a sense, an inventor himself. He felt an enthusiasm comparable to that of the speaker he had heard. But the task of convincing and creating enthusiasm in the patient was another matter. He could find no acceptable source in the libraries or among his colleagues. He ended up taking a course in meditation from a 23 year old "uncredentialled" boy. "I was extremely skeptical, thought their claims were ridiculous, also that the course was far too expensive." (Obviously, he had stumbled into a greedy outfit.) "In spite of the instructor's youth and lack of credentials and all my skepticism, taking this course was like being shot out of a sling shot ... It was as if all the work I had gone through to learn to teach attitude to patients had been put together in this class."

His first patient was a 61 year old man to whom he explained the medical treatment to be applied and also how, through mutual imagery, they were going to attempt to affect his disease. This man could at that time eat no food, could barely swallow his own saliva. 'I had him relax three times a day, mentally picturing his disease, his treatment and the way his body was interacting with the treatment and the disease, so that he could better understand his disease and cooperate with what. was going on. The results were amazing. When I explained to my colleagues what I was doing, they said to me, jokingly, 'Why do you even bother to turn on the machine?' My response to that was, 'I just don't know enough yet.'

"This patient was described in the fall of 1972 as being "a year and a half post-treatment, with no evidence of cancer in his throat.' He also had arthritis and he used the same basic mental processes and eliminated that. He also had trouble with impotence. He had been impotent for over 20 years. It took him 10 days of relaxing and mentally picturing this problem and the solution in his mind's eye and he was able to resume intercourse with his wife. He now states he is able to have intercourse two or three times a week. When he called me and told me of resolving his impotence, I had him explain how he did it, just in case I should need the technique later in my own life."

Before going on to more striking case histories, the connection between full employment and cancer should be noted. Today's worker and, particularly, the highly developed researcher lives in constant fear that his work will be interrupted by whimsical decisions "for reasons of economy (! ! !)" so all his work may be in vain and his precious family may suffer, perhaps starve. For one not trained in mind preservation, such fear causes cancer by a chance of, say, 50%. The average man may be less apt to worry, so his chance of cancer is slightly less.

Generally speaking, then, unemployment is a major cause of cancer. Reversely expressed: Full employment is a cancer cure. Mind training is a cure for both cancer and unemployment. By building a generation bridge from himself to a 23 year old "uncredentialled boy", Dr. Simonton discovered this.

Then, as he was through with his first patient, he was drafted. He was upset, for he thought he would not be able to go on with this work in the military. But fate favored him: He was sent to Travis Air Force Base and made head of a brand new department. He explained his basic approach to his commanding officer, General Reynolds, who was very receptive. The Air Force, with its General Reynolds and Colonel Mrazek, seems to be a pioneer in advanced medicine.

Dr. Simonton's first patient at Travis was a nonsmoking navigator who had a squamous carcinoma in the roof of his mouth and a larger one at the back of his throat. The cancer in the roof of his mouth should have had a cure rate of 30 to 50% the one in his throat 5 to 40%. Collectively, however, the estimated cure rate would probably be no more than 5 to 10%, since two cancers at the same time worsen the situation.

This was an extremely positive patient, very cooperative. After one week, the tumor was beginning to shrink. After four weeks the ulceration had no growth evidence. "It was generally outside my experience to get such dramatic response in two separate tumors in such a short time. After a month there was one small ulceration, healing nicely, and after about ten weeks the roof of his mouth was essentially normal in appearance. The truly beautiful thing was that the lesion in the throat showed the same response as the one in the mouth and, on routine examination, it was impossible to tell where the throat tumor had been. Only three months after he had been taken off flying status this man had unanimous clearance from the head and neck tumor board to go back on flying status and resume his profession.

Another case involved a wart on a man's index finger. The wart had been treated for a year and had become progressively worse on all types of medical management. The man was brought back from Vietnam for amputation of the finger, because of the pain. He also had a wart on the thumb of the opposite hand that the Travis base was not planning to treat initially. They were going to see if the immune mechanism would be stimulated by treating of the first wart.

The patient was very receptive. As the wart on the index finger was treated, the second wart responded with a one and one half day's delay. After one month's treatment there was essentially no evidence of any warty tissue on either finger.

A third case was a 55 year old woman with a large anal carcinoma. She had an extensive tumor and large clinically positive inguinal nodes that had not been biopsied. The tumor successively decreased in size. After three weeks most of the gross tumor was gone. After four and a half weeks there was no gross evidence of tumor and the enlargement of the lymph nodes had nearly completely disappeared without treatment. After six more weeks she was virtually totally healed.

The first fifty persons treated at Travis were divided into attitude groups, from negative to positive, averaged out from independent evaluations by five staff members. Only four out of the fifty were considered as having poor response. Twelve were considered excellent. Five of these had less than 50% chance for a cure. Thirty-seven had either good or excellent response.

Lastly, Dr. Simonton writes about young patients from homes where communication between family members had been so poor that the patients felt unloved. The doctor then included the whole family in his consultation and treatment, and found that it was not love that had been lacking but understanding. The family members had been unable to build those generation bridges. So those predisposed to illness became seriously ill. Dr. Simonton, using his unique experience and driven by his unusually strong desire to help, then became the expert engineer, fixing up those bridges-the same kind we need, and sometimes have, between groupings and professions in our society.

After all this success Dr. Simonton admits, "The most difficult person for me to convince as to the validity of my work has been my father." His father was very ill and needed his son's help. Finally even that was overcome.*

* The above is condensed from *The Dimensions of Healing* by the gracious permission of The Academy of Parapsychology and Healing in Los Altos, California.

Vendettas and Morality

"Morals," said Bernard Shaw, "is suspecting your neighbors of not being legally married."

"Morals," said an American teenager, "is a noble art practiced between two persons who know each other's needs."

The latter kind of morals has a lot to do with a nation's economy and social stability. Another word for it is consideration. The consideration must also be shown by the community in not interfering with its members' behavior when this behavior is tempered by consideration to all sides. The community should protect its members from attack and coercion but not prescribe behavior.

In the American community we are lucky to be able to practice monogamy, a deeply satisfying though challenging social custom which seems to suit our majority, and which could not be practiced in ancient Arabia where males died like flies in wars and vendettas and there was such a surplus of women that to make love and motherhood available to most, men had to marry many wives. Conversely, in modern Tibet the men are in a majority and women marry several men. Some women often marry all the brothers of one family.

In the present American society many consider the monogamistic family the basis of our social structure, its atom. Two units, man and woman, voluntarily unite into one. If substantial numbers of these voluntary units are broken, by divorce, for example, does not the entire social pattern face collapse?

Not if consideration has been shown or at least sincerely tried. But if a man writes-as one recently did in a national magazine, "My wife became ill, could no longer satisfy me, so I had to leave her and seek my happiness elsewhere," doesn't he suspect he is doing his bit to dissolve our society as it is today? Whatever business security he still enjoyed , whatever income he could carry safely home, whatever fruits of our civilization he still enjoyed - doesn't he suspect all these things were due, not to himself any longer but to those others, who still field together the fine threads of which our communities are built, who wouldn't just leave a sick mate? The man of conscience, the man who can see beyond his car, and the freeway, not merely obeys the law but adds other laws of his own making.

Why did this man write that article in the first place? No doubt to defend himself against neighbors who disagreed with him and, above all, against himself. And why did the editor print it? To air a most interesting and vital subject and to give the man a chance to plead his cause. This is the case with so many articles and books which are misinterpreted by outsiders as portraying a callous moral standard. The opposite is true. These things are read with interest because they are unusual, because the reader tests these aberrations against his own life and meaning, against a marriage, perhaps, that, aided and abetted by consideration and togetherness, developed beyond his wildest hopes.

From his mountain of happiness he may even doubt the validity of polls. Some teenage girls have told him about poll-takers from scientific study groups asking them about their sex lives and those who said they had none, that they were waiting for marriage, were just stricken off the list, considered liars.

In today's discussions, including statistics, ("Statistics can be used to support anything, particularly statisticians.") toughness is often preferred over truth and it is forgotten that a young girl, who has been permitted to grow like a flower, also belongs to the human race. At her first awakening of a liking, a fondness, she tries to cover her feelings, even to herself. To the civilized sexist, she is a square and he may shout it in her ear because her beautiful innocence makes her doubly desirable. He blames her unresponse on "the old morals", not knowing that teenager's definition or that no society ever had any old or new morals, but that this word means an art practiced between people who feel each other's need. To such people statistics are flat. They do not look to the community for moral rules, although they may appreciate society's protection against the inconsiderate. Though even this is dubious as long as society does not permit each man to satisfy his urges by offering him a valid chance to earn, each day, his and his family's bread.

Oh? Since when did this become society's duty?

Since about fifty years ago in the United States. This was when a haphazard association of people became welded into a technological dragon abundantly able to take care of any one willing to lend a hand or brain, however limited. Peter F. Drucker, teaching management at the New York University, thinks we are now about to realize this (*Harvard Business Review*, November-December '69):

"Within another ten years we will become far less concerned with management development (that is, adapting the individual to the demands of the organization), and far more with organization development (that is, adapting the company to the needs, aspirations and potentials of individuals)."

Delaying this sound development are such current lamentations,

"A core of unemployables will always be with us since some cannot acquire the talents needed in our cybernetic working place." Obviously these people do not know much about "our cybernetic working place".

Americans who trained Hindu and Vietnam peasants to become efficient plumbers and mechanics already applied Peter Drucker's second principle, adapting their task to the needs, aspirations and potentials of their charges. Lockheed Aircraft Company did it here at home; gambled on two efforts at once (*Harvard Business Review* September-October 1968). Near Atlanta, Georgia, a group was employed of which sixty-three percent had records; seventy-three percent were of racial or national minority groups; sixty percent had previously been on welfare; only fifteen percent had ever been industrially employed before; medium age was twenty-six; thirty percent were married. The other group was at Sunnyvale, California; seventy-six percent of these people had been on welfare; forty percent had police records; only twenty percent had ever been industrially employed, medium age was twenty-six; eighty-two percent were heads of households. They had on an average ten years' education.

Length of training was twelve weeks for the first group (sheet metal) and four weeks for the second group (odd jobs, though some became key-punch operators, electrical assemblers). Seventy-eight entered training in the first group and forty-three worked. In the second group one hundred eleven entered training and one hundred eight worked.

The turnover record was better for these hard-core "unemployables" than for the company's average, and one supervisor commented, "Best trained and most productive men I've ever received!" Another comment, "These men (and women) really want to work; they work hard and the quality of their work is very good."

The training was based on continuous demonstrations and repetitions. The instructors concluded that all training ought to be conducted in this fashion. The requirements during training were aimed slightly higher than strictly necessary for the jobs to be performed. This increased confidence and improved performance and this, too, was considered a hint. for future training in general.

These people had definite jobs to look forward to all through their training. which was specifically tailored to these jobs - a far safer and better procedure than general training which may or may not result in a job not yet defined.

These trainees appeared more eager to succeed, more dedicated than the average influx of employees, thus spiking the contention that "unemployables" would be improperly motivated.

The two Lockheed groups were small but they started a trend. Not all following efforts were as successful as Lockheed's, though one more recent try was even more successful. The Bell System Companies of New Jersey hired 173 "hard-core unemployables". A June 1970 report quotes the drop-out rate for this category at four percent while the rate for regular male employees hired during the same period was forty-three percent. Some had uncorrectable visual defects, some asthma, some had had hearing problems and some atrophied limbs. Several were suspected of using narcotics. Every one flunked the group test that Bell gives to all applicants. They were nevertheless employed-as truck drivers, coin box collectors, even as business machine operators or at crafts or technical work. It was concluded that the company's aptitude tests had unnecessarily screened out acceptable candidates. G.P. Bisgeier, Medical Director of the New Jersey Bell Telephone Company, reported, "The Group Record is surprisingly good."

In *The Choices We Face*, Lyndon Baines Johnson's compact overview of his Presidential period, he reports his talks with Henry Ford II about a pilot project of private firms hiring "unemployables" in our fifty largest cities. At the end of 1968 he estimated that twenty-two million Americans were still "very poor". So we haven't come far. The miniscule successes are still important. They pinpoint the potentials.

A Foreign Aid veteran commented, "We, who trained Hindus and Vietnamese to become plumbers and mechanics, knew the principles of thorough demonstrations and repetitions that also secured Lockheed's and Bell's successes. Much sooner than we expected, our trainees turned around and helped us. And, like Bell, we ignored the usual tests and educational requirements. Lockheed first set a fifth grade reading ability as condition for employment, then found this unnecessary and lowered the entrance condition to second grade reading. In India and Vietnam there were no entrance requirements at all. This, I hope, shall eventually apply everywhere."

More important than employment in existing enterprises is search for and development of entrepreneurial talents, so more people may establish and run their own firms. In the May-June 1970 *Harvard Business Review* Michael Brower and Doyle Little extensively review *Black Capitalism*. This is defined as "Black" ownership, management and control of productive profit-seeking organizations. Since black participation along such has been relatively low, the search for more black capitalism has become a national goal and is overwhelmingly endorsed within the largest corporations. What is sought are not small, marginal businesses, or exploitation of poor black workers by a few rich black capitalists, but sizeable businesses owned widely by workers and residents of a community, or a broadly controlled community development corporation. A growing number of large companies have established programs to develop such minority businesses, with investments ranging from $10,000 to $300,000. More companies are making a point of buying from black businesses.

There is a prospect of much larger involvement when the art of finding and developing competent black management will have become better understood. With few exceptions, corporations have not been too successful in choosing either black managers or temporary white managers for new black businesses. Better management has been selected when white sponsoring corporations worked with black community development organizations that did the search, screening and selection of management, good results were also obtained when black entrepreneurs sought out the white corporations, rather than waiting for the initiative to come from the latter. Generally, people with previous managerial experience, either in large industries or in their own small enterprises, did better than, for example, teachers or government workers without managerial experience.

While concrete results are, so far, few and far between, there is determination from both sides to make this work. It is a real and coming thing, particularly when the multisurveys planned by the Kennedy people will be resumed and followed by economic expansion with ample means available for what we want to do. In the same May-June number of *Harvard Business Review*, Dean S. Ammer writes about *The Side Effects of Planning*, showing how the increasingly frequent "three-year plans" and "five-year plans" of private businesses influence the entire national economy. Some may wonder whether we are copying socialist planning when we speak of three or five-year plans. There is a crucial difference. The five-year plans of American firms keep strictly to the well-known area of each particular firm and do not build bureaucratic fantasy structures upon insufficient information.

The effects of these five-year plans in the community in general is to stabilize the economy while at the same time keeping tuned to technological changes - the same effect that the Kennedy surveys would have. Additionally, these five - and- three -year plans would form an excellent preparation and foundation for the larger survey planned by the Kennedy group and explained in the last chapter.

We have displayed the tantalizing prospective goodies - for whose benefit? The monogamistic couple, community's atom, at their mountain of happiness? Or the henpecked and the nagging? Fools laugh at Abraham Lincoln and Socrates and their wife trouble, forgetting that these great men gave their mates what nobody else could. Apart from that, with more ample incomes the nagging might recede. Or the child, in whom the couple and parent merge, isn't it a worthy receiver? For what can all the love in the world and all religions do for a mother who doesn't have money to feed her child? But through our surveys and efforts, the community may be given the means to feed all mothers and their children, which will prove cheaper in the end.

Here religion enters again, or seems to enter, through the back door of statistics, which indicates that divorce rates are lower - in one count as low as one to one hundred and twenty five - among people deeply devoted to a religious ideal, as compared to one to five for others. Additionally, community spirit and distribution of food and necessities are smoother, avoiding crisis, in religious groups.

However, religion alone is not enough to provide a sound and efficient economic structure. There must also be knowledge - for example, knowledge of how money is created or destroyed in our modern community. A community's daily activities create and destroy money. When a business man borrows from a bank, a myriad of new deposits are developed through accounting and banking practices, more so if business in general is booming. Also, when the Government borrows money through a bond issue, and cannot sell all of these bonds to the public, it offers the rest to certain banks. As a result, new deposits are created in the books of the nation. We have more money in our hands are funding more businesses, more jobs - until, eventually, the banks may sell these bonds or some of them to their clients. That may, or may not reduce the money in circulation, depending on what these clients do with their bonds.

Ouch! Now some think we may just as well create as much money as we seem to need in this manner. Creating too much may be as dangerous as strangling the supply. Two things must be considered before a businessman will ask for a loan and before a bank will grant it: Will the loan serve to produce goods that can be sold for a profit? And, are there workers and equipment available to produce those goods or services?

The first question may be answered by a survey. So far a market analysis has been sufficient. Now we have come to a point where a more sophisticated, more comprehensive national survey of the whole field of science, technology, manpower and desires is required. Before such a survey has been undertaken, no bank and no government truly knows what we can afford. Such a comprehensive survey was planned during the Kennedy Administration and shall be briefly described in the concluding chapter.

The question of available labor is controversial, as a previous discussion hinted. The solution to this problem was one of the purposes of the survey planned during the Kennedy Administration.

Now my burglarious mind is invading a convoy leader's mind, as it was in World War II. It wants to tell about an innovation, eagerly, proudly. The general rule, it says, was to tell the convoy drivers to keep in touch with the vehicle ahead. They did - and lost the ones behind, who often had to wait for crossing traffic. Large chunks of the convoys were cut off for hours, days, sometimes were never found.

Our American society, he says, is like these convoy drivers looking obediently ahead, not back or to the sides. So we are losing not only the marginals, the "unemployables", the millions we misjudged "unfit", but in addition our balance, or sense, and our organization.

One day, our friend had his turn as a convoy leader. He reversed the order of the day: Drivers, look back. Look ahead too, but be sure to keep in touch with the vehicle behind you. From then on, all vehicles arrived together. Order, sanity, cohesion were restored.

Lastly, I venture a jump to that Yogi haven, the Himalayas. On my way to Badrinath, that holiest of shrines, I arrived with the pilgrim crowd at Bela Kushi. We were told our car would take us all the way to Joshimath. How could that be? Before us was the foaming, frothing Aknanda River crossed by nothing better than a fragile, swaying footbridge.

What did these local drivers do? Without a moment's hesitation, they jumped from their seats, ripped their tool kits from the trunks, took the cars apart, ran across the swaying footbridge with the parts in their rucksack, assembled the cars on the other bank. No sooner was the last nut tight than the drivers jumped into their seats again and drove confidently on to Joshimath. They could not write their names in a single language. They didn't know one word of English. Yet, in a few weeks, Americans had taught them to be assemblers as good as the best in Detroit.

Reading and writing are two of the most overrated qualifications. And what about enthusiasm? Perhaps these Hindu auto assemblers had more of it than some Americans who have lost their hope through generations of mismanagement.

This means it may take a little longer here. That is all.

THE GOOD SAMARITAN AND COMPUTERS

Computers, lie detectors and good Samaritans sway people, their communities, economics. Those super sleuths, who know everything, told us that President Truman didn't fire General MacArthur before he had consulted the computer. The computer was asked whether we could, at that time, afford a war as big as MacArthur proposed. The computer said no. So there it was. The electronic wizard had spoken.

The electronic wizard has spoken again, about the war in Vietnam.

Dr. Norbert Wiener, the so-charming and unassuming father of all computers, visited the University of California just before he passed away. We were anxious to talk to him (the "we" is not here used for "Majesty") not the least about his recent statement that computers might usurp men's decisions. How could he, of all people, say that man-made and man-fed machines could extend beyond man's wish and will?

"Of course not," he smiled, oh, so engagingly, "Except for man's superstition."

Just because computers can do some things faster, some believe they can also do things better, that they have better judgment.

All a computer can do is magnify our speed, the speed with which we make mistakes, for example. The alluring feature which deludes the unwary is that this speed permits a computer to quickly assimilate and coordinate many various thought patterns. If these thought patterns were not all true (and how could all of them be true?) then the coordinated sum total is untrue also.

The "lie detector" is a striking and shocking example. If not exactly a computer, it is a horribly misused machine. At the Berkeley campus of the University of California, in the mid-fifties, a student was suspected of murder. One morning the papers sported a statement by a policeman,

"A lie detector test shows that our man is guilty."

With the complete backing of the then-head of the university's Law Department, I phoned this policeman. "Your instrument shows nothing but emotions. If you repeat to a suspect the same question you have already thrust at him a hundred times, how can he help being upset, outraged, and register what you misinterpret as guilt?"

The terse reply came gruffly, "How many lie detector tests have you conducted?"

My reply to that was not conciliatory. "If I had employed your device, even once, with serious intent, I would have considered myself disqualified."

I added, "J. Edgar Hoover happens to be in my corner, you know."

"I know. I also know the reason for Edgar Hoover's viewpoint."

Since no solution was in prospect with this gentleman, I went to the Chief of Police, offered to undergo a lie detector test in his presence, at which I would make the machine call me a liar when I was telling the plain truth, and register "True!" when I told screaming lies. This is easy for anyone knowing how this machine is made. This holds true for the simple version and for the most sophisticated type. Suave, intelligent criminals and particularly spies know this and can easily "handle" the machine. Nevertheless, even Allen Dulles used it when he was head of the Central Intelligence Agency. This deeply troubled General Mark Clark who investigated the CIA and mused that if a baby wet itself while under the spell of a lie detector, big amplitudes would interpret its emotions as uncouth lying.

The police chief sweetly assured me he might consider my offer, though only "after we've settled this murder case."

This false faith in computers and lie detectors is part of a wider human frailty:

We ascribe miraculous powers, or evil intent, to persons or things we don't know. We see people of a different color, different traits walking down the street. We conjure up amazing fictional characteristics and hang them on to these people.

In the same vein, a policeman may have conducted lie detector tests most of his life without the slightest knowledge of what his detector actually shows. "It works!" he jubilates after having tried it on a hundred naive offenders who still squirm when they tell a lie. He forgets, does not even notice when the machine plunges innocents into the cruelest fates or sets free a smart aleck.

As of now, the lie detector is spreading its ugly lies all over Washington, D.C. where several large Departments subject all their employees above a certain rank to this "test".

Similarly, our dispositions in the most complex war in our history were influenced by computers excelling in multiplying the mistakes of political or military strategists.

With such goings-on in our government, what can we expect of our youth?

There is an old story about a man who was beaten and mauled and was lying in the street, helpless. Many passed by, looking the other way; some because the beaten man wasn't of their race; others simply because they couldn't be bothered.

Then a Samaritan came by, a man of an entirely different race and build. So, obviously, he must be an incompetent. Yet, this stranger stopped and helped the wounded man.

Is this just a story about different religions, different races in a far-off land far back in time?

It would be comfortable to think so. To some of us, the story of this beaten man and the Samaritan is the story of the computer and the lie detector here and now. That student at the University of California was worse than beaten. He was stamped a murderer. His trial was dominated by jurors with superstitions about lie detectors.

Another modern superstition condemns millions - not to death, but to unemployment, which is not much better. Practically everybody will tell you that full employment equates inflation. What is inflation? What is a little inflation and what is a big inflation, and what relation is there between the two, if any? The final chapter reviews such economic finery. Here, we shall just quote Leon H. Keyserling, a man not to be ignored in these fields, who doubts that even a little inflation needs to follow full employment. In *The Problem of Problems*, the beginning article in *Social Policies for America in the Seventies* (1968), he writes,

"The experience since 1953 had already, in the main (and still has), refuted any direct and positive correlation between the rate of price inflation and the rate of economic growth or our degree of closeness to reasonable full resource uses."

He adds, "In any event, how can we accept the proposition that we should foist unemployment upon breadwinners and their families in the millions in order to insure the affluent that they will not have to pay somewhat higher prices for their third cars, fur coats and steak dinners?"

Some of my generation, like Leon Keyserling and John Philip Wernette, are raring to go. Are there enough of them? Among the young I find more, but will they keep their fire through the ordeal of education and early life?

Enthusiastic youth, are you ready to tackle, master and revise the messy world you inherited from your elders? After having been schooled in all our tricks, the clean ones and the unclean ones, our knowledge and our ignorance?

Why do you think you will do so much better than we did?

Of course you will. You have bigger, newer computers (some of the newer ones don't work well, I hear, so we have to go back to older ones). You have color television (which takes away another dimension of your individual imagination substituting TV writers' imagination and brains). You have Lasers (upon each beam a hundred million units of telephone chatter are conveyed, further dissipating your energy and drive). You have microfilms of great books and many more small books by means of which your mind and heart are distracted and diminished.

Yes, cybernetically, you will be doing better.

And what about those ancient tales? Could they add or subtract?

That tale about the good Samaritan added a lot - to my pain; also to my understanding, I hope. All those ancient tales could add, or subtract, or go by you without a trace depending on your own knowledge and your attitude. And now, instead of painting abstract word pictures, we shall look at the shining example of Bishop James A. Pike for whom the ancient tales meant so much that he devoted his life to them while he was also well aware of cybernetics and its applications to modern law. The fact, however, that makes him particularly suitable is that his honesty meant more to him than smoothness, truth more than peace. He brings to mind Bernard Shaw's words, "The reasonable man changes himself to suit the world; the unreasonable one insists upon trying to change the world. All progress, therefore, is due to the unreasonable man."

It also helps that with all his great knowledge, Bishop Pike shows eddies of ignorance; for example when he attacks Trinity, which is an old, very significant symbol for the observer, the observed and observation. This will be elaborated in a following chapter. Bishop Pike is right that Trinity, as now taught in churches, could easily derail you. (In the Middle Ages people were burned at the stake for saying God was one, not three.) But, without an accompanying explanation of where the concept came from, one is left dangling in the air or, as has been said about Bishop Pike, he has one foot in the stream and one on dry land. This endears him to people and makes him so human. Greater waves were raised by his statement that, "the concept of Jesus being the son of God is not useful."

Here the prelate mind unites with the stringent lawyer mind. Lawyer Pike knows it is useless to argue whether or not Jesus really was the son of God (and the only son!) for who ever defined God or the son of God? And how could a man with a lawyer's mind argue about words no one could define? To ponder whether the concept is useful or not is another matter-useful for mind and heart; useful for sound development. To assume that the followers of one faith have access to the one and only real son of God - can such a belief be useful? Or is it conceited, crude, ugly, brutal and destructive of international relations and peace, let alone truth?

To compassionate students of ancient tales there is another meaning for this concept: That we are all sons or daughters of God who created us. There is this further feeling that some of us are more true sons, or at least more alert and keen sons, recognizing the sonship more than others. Those who view sonship in this light, who say they feel Jesus was a keener and more alert son than most, have a useful sonship concept.

So, through his penetrating and often violent and sometimes partially ignorant crash attacks, Bishop Pike leads us up the path to more wisdom and a wider scope of mutual respect and even love. In a sense, he divides us into three groups: The persistent believers, not in the ancient tales themselves but in the interpretations their sect has supplied. These people converse and operate well with those who believe exactly as they do. To others their hearts and minds are closed whether they live next door or in China. So they are only half-awake in the body of humanity. The story of the good Samaritan beckons to them, but do they notice?

The second group rejects all ancient tales. Toward the believers their reactions vary from a shrug to pity to amusement to condescending tolerance. They have fun among themselves at parties and at work and they may get along fairly well in this world. Yet their minds are half-closed, closed to all the beauty and wisdom the ancient tales have in store for the open mind. Closed, also, to all those people who live by or with those ancient tales. So they contribute to the isolation that causes all the unpleasantnesses among us - and that caused a Samaritan to act.

There is the third group, open to all sides, laughing with the laughing, bowing with the bowing, though never fearing, never subjecting themselves to superstition or - one might say - never thoughtlessly believing and never disbelieving.

Is there anything more sobering or more satisfying than breaking the chain of your immediate surroundings and your own mind and finding a new and wider world communication with more people? Whatever path one chooses, there are always powerful hands to help one along, the hands of the good Samaritans.

A Symbol is an Ocean in a Drop

The United States, whose citizens hail from all corners of the world, has absorbed the widest variety of gold nuggets or butterflies of wisdom, hidden in the symbols that thrill, embolden and inspire men. To touch this community, its economics and employment, for example, one might wish to delve into this treasure chest.

Many see the symbol of the cross as a backbone of a great tale, an object of reverence, reminding one of suffering for a mighty cause. Its earlier history was lighter, more playful: The vertical line symbolized your rapid rise, prompted by your ambition. Then a horizontal line, representing the requirements of others, of your community, challenged and often delayed your upward rise. But this broadened your scope, and you grew in a new direction. You became wider-ranging, nobler - a resurrection.

A boy wishes to avoid supervision and authority, he wishes to roam the countryside and raid apple orchards, while a seemingly heartless community of elders requires him to go to school and to curb his greed and limit his enjoyment to the petty proceeds from his parental allowance.

His immediate reaction is resentment. He tries to escape, by ruse or war. The years that follow by and by bring home to him that the community is the soil in which he grows and, whatever its faults, taught him consideration, expanded his consciousness, enriched him. The cross becomes his Joy.

When anyone, religious or not, has a tough problem, a need for self-control, wise decisions and unforeseen expenses, he says "Well, this is the cross I have to bear." Mysteriously, he feels a little better; later again much better; and he has more courage, for he feels there is a "happy ending" with the cross; a vital significance.

A symbol from ancient Hindu traditions has been adopted by large sections of Christianity in a different and strange sense. This is the symbol of the trinity. Originally, it was just a mental distinction of certain facts: the seer, the seen, the sight; the Creator, his creation and the process of creation; God the Creator and source of all religions, his "son" or prophet receiving and interpreting the inspiration, the inspiration itself or the "Holy Ghost".

The idea of trinity, then, is not a dogma to be believed and quarrelled about, but a voluntary classification of mental pictures. The purpose of this classification is clarifying these pictures and their mutual relationship. There are other applications too. The idea is often symbolized by an equilateral triangle.

Life was pictured as the waters of a sea in the ancient traditions of philosophy and religion, particularly in the Middle East. When the storms and waves of the sea of life overpowered you so you couldn't stay with it, you were said to drown. When you barely made it, you were said to swim. When your philosophical and loving attitude completely mastered the difficulties and challenges of life, you were said to walk upon the waters. To calm and harmonize the minds and emotions of oneself or others was called to still the storm. To improve the taste of the ordinary life of hard knocks and blows by a loving and compassionate attitude was called to turn the water of life into wine.

In the Holy Eucharist, wine is given as a symbol of Divine Love. The wine is also thought of as the blood of God. With the wine is given bread, a symbol of Divine Knowledge. The bread is also thought of as the body of God.

He who gave up blood on a cross poured tragedy, actual drama into the philosophical symbol and impressed even those who would not have been interested in the subtle and real significance.

Before the crucifixion, as a symbol of the coming event, he gave his disciples bread to eat and wine to drink "which is my flesh and blood". He wanted to tell them that Divine Knowledge and Divine

Love was his real flesh and blood - the real flesh and blood of every man rather than the physical molecules of the body.

The bread and wine also symbolizes the well-knit structure of this universe and that even such a flimsy thing as Love is more substantial than we first think, at least as substantial as wine, and that all we eat and drink and feel and think is from that same one source which we may call GOD. Now we know that love is also steam, electricity, atomic power.

Blood donors give of their physical blood for transfusion to sick fellowmen. Simultaneously, they give generous thoughts and good wishes. They receive in due time a corresponding amount of blood from the workshop of nature in their own bodies - and, so, also love, inspiration and generous thoughts in exchange for those they gave, and the latter much faster than the physical blood.

To the enthusiasts, this all points to a climax: That this whole world is held together and run by love, the vibration, bundles of love. Love? How can one explain war in Vietnam then - and riots in Detroit?

Well, the great scheme of love hasn't quite penetrated yet. Not every man is fully clear about it, not yet. God may be perfect potentially, in time, though not quite yet - if God is everything. If He is everything, then he has a few miles to go yet - through and with all of us.

The story of Jesus, his son, is the story of one, anyone, in the forefront. Eventually, it will be the story of all.

Some people brazenly proclaim the exclusive greatness of Jesus, the man or the God. This man himself said, "Call me not good. Only One is good, that is God!" which seems to mean that his message was not for glorifying one man. It was concerned with the Spirit embodying all men. The greatness is in the Spirit. If so, this is good news for the Spirit is always with us. It is expressed in individuals, in nature, in the whole universe, in oneself.

If Buddha seems the perfect expression of the Spirit to some, Jesus to others, how could one be pronounced greater than the other? How could the Spirit be greater than itself? Who could feel capable of comparing and judging them, thus proclaiming themselves greater than either?

Measuring the greatness of men and comparing them belongs to the world of separateness below the spirit level. In the world of the Spirit, there are no measurements, no comparisons. All are like flutes of reed through which the Spirit plays its music.

There is breathtaking beauty in the symbol and fact of the immaculate conception. Each child is more than just flesh and blood. Before birth, the mother has been overshadowed by God's holy spirit and while the earthly father and mother provide the physical frame, God breathes into life the soul. It seems such a pity, then, that so many souls are born into festering ghettoes and can see no great promise in their physical existence. Churches have been watching this spectacle for ages with greater patience than concern.

Immaculate conception is operating not only among humans but in all the huge and tiny explosive events we call creation. Two forces were always involved: positive and negative, male and female, ying and yang, jelal and jemal. The irresistible positive and male force overshadows and fuses with the negative - the female - the jemal being, and new beings spring to life. On February 14, 1637, one such new life, mothered by Madame d'Aiguemere of France, was adjudged by three medical experts to have been born by real immaculate conception. This verdict was upheld by the Paris Supreme Court after the latter had called in several more experts.

Whatever the procedures, as the earth is made fertile by rays of the sun and as the moon takes light from the sun and gives out heat and light in its turn, so a woman takes on a ray of the Spirit along with conception and, in due time, bears a soul with a body-frame.

Heaven and Hell, mean, to some, names of places they go to after death. To others, "Heaven" is that state of mind a person may enjoy here on earth as a result of pure thoughts and emotions and proper acts. "Hell" is the opposite state of mind. In this sense, Heaven and Hell are symbols. They are single words producing a series of mental pictures different and characteristic for each individual.

Heaven and Hell, like other words we throw around, are not areas to be "found" but conditions we make - and later unmake - if we so choose. Conditions, surroundings master us only as long as we let them. The purpose of life is for us to master or adjust to conditions, surroundings - and ourselves. For that purpose we were made.

Atonement is practiced in shipyards and on football fields as happily as in the tale.

A shipyard may turn out seaworthy craft in record time and be the pride of the nation though two shipfitters played hookey. The rest of the workers, including the designers, made up for the hookey so honorably that the net result was rousing. The able and industrious workers atone for the sins of the hookey-players. The slackers may be taken through a training course and may become as conscientious and efficient as the best without even knowing very clearly how they were before. They have been saved by their betters.

On the football field it is, of course, a bit different in that a critical public is usually armed with spoiled tomatoes, rotten eggs and empty coca-coca bottles and let the off-key players have it. Even so, the net play may turn out well in spite of the unfortunate targets.

Since the shipyard and the football field are nothing but true reflections of the Spirit World, the rules and the laws are the same. The group as a whole has to reap as it sowed, but not always the individuals - who may be saved by the grace and wish of those ahead.

What are prayers? Asking favors? To some they are just that. Others live their lives in constant prayer although they want no favors, they think of nothing but giving. To such, a prayer is tuning the mind and heart to the vibrations of the Spirit. Prayer is leading one's thoughts and emotions along a certain path. Then one may wish to stop at choice points of beauty and take in the view. This is called meditation or contemplation. There is no agreed difference between these two words although some consider meditation more or less haphazard thinking as compared to the more concentrated attention which they term contemplation. Concentration these same people define as focusing your thought - on anything. When you focus on

God or any religious concept, then, only, they say, do you meditate or contemplate. All three activities lift the mind and heart above the daily chores, worries, fears or grudges, and make one receptive to inspiration.

Those who study the physical aspect of thoughts and feelings - as far as they may be studied at this time (New discoveries are made almost daily and during the time it takes to have this printed and brought to the shelves, we may know vastly more. . .) - feel that prayer and contemplation affect not only he who prays but spread throughout the universe as bundles of vibrations, like all other mental and emotional activities affecting with varying strength all other minds and hearts. Many religious people always believed this and, so, prayed in the solitude of monastaries or mountain caves to help, not only themselves but others as well. This influence on others may not always have come up to the expectations of the pious and is not usually a good enough excuse for running away from the world. The urge to run away, to seek long periods of complete solitude often stems from fear or over-sensitivity. Before acting, a look at oneself and a sober evaluation may be in order. But this looking should be exercised by oneself, not by others.

The Nazarene never permitted himself long sessions of solitude. The suffering of people around him kept him in their midst. Similarly, in the *Bhagavad Gita*, the most popular (in the West) of the holy books of India, the Lord's advice to his disciple, Arjuna, is not to abandon his worldly duties, not to give in to his urge to quit the coming battle but - while retaining his prayerful attitude - to go in there and fight.

Life in this world with its responsibilities, wars, worries and jarring influences, was made by man, for man, for his spiritual awakening and evolution, and is not to be shunned by him who wants to know and grow. There is no progress for him in leaving this world for the luxury of solitude - except for occasional refreshments. There is no sweeter fragrance than of prayers rising from the work bench or the din of battle.

COMMUNICATORS

Communication, to some, means language, which, they feel, is coterminous with human life. Jagjit Singh, with tongue in cheek, quotes a contrasting viewpoint in his *Information Theory, Language and Cybernetics*: "The word remains upon the speaker's lips and refuses to go and rest upon the thing, making language an absurd medley of sounds and symbols beyond which flows the world - an indiscriminate and uncommunicable chaos."

Most of us drop occasionally into such a cynical cesspool, then rise again to exuberant praises of linguistic communication when we come under the spell of a good teacher.

There are some, however, who maintain continuous reserve about language communication, even though they talk quite sensibly when they do talk. I had a friend, Inayat Khan, a musician from India, with a keen sensitivity to human feelings and attitudes. He thought twice before ever expressing his ideas or feelings, which, he said, might have an effect entirely different from what you intended.

He called himself a mystic. He fondled this word. He said it simply means a communicator, one who always communicates, either through or beyond words. We did some work together, which often caused me to criticize him, his associates, his methods. That is, in the beginning I criticized. He never answered with words. He just smiled, and instead of harsh sounds came subtle thoughts floating through the space between us and, bit by bit, I read them so well that, with him at least, I began to employ the same "language".

Is this what may be called diplomacy? Not the kind defined as saying the nastiest things in the nicest way, but a real diplomacy of the heart?

Isn't cybernetics supposed to take care of that? Indirectly, it has helped by showing up our lack of skill, lack of real feelings, showing up all this in a grotesquely exaggerated output. If cybernetics hasn't reformed us, it is beginning to urge us to reform ourselves.

In a class by itself are the new gadgets that register not words or equations, but feelings. The most famous and most notorious of these is the lie detector, which does register feelings and physiological reactions to feelings. That these have been assumed to translate truth or falsehood is a sorry short-circuit in the current of thought and understanding. When, some day, the magnitude of feelings related to truth or falsehood becomes better known, we shall laugh and cry at our once-upon-a-time delusions.

From humanity's dawn, millenniums before cybernetics were thought of, though often using the same trends of thought, some individuals and groups reached amazing feats of communication. Periodically, they closed their mouths and shut off communication by the senses and directed their attention inward, to their own thoughts and feelings, seeking there understanding of themselves, and thereby understanding of and with others, even communication with others. Ancient tales and some modern ones tell about people so full of love and of such ardent desire that they penetrated the barriers dividing us and saw, felt, knew other minds. They were called mystics, meaning fakers to some, communicators to others.

An oft-quoted meaning of mystic is "shutter" (Greek), referring to the mystics' shutting their mouths and gazing inwards. To language enthusiasts such behavior seems weirdly unprofitable since speaking is their proof of human qualities. Therefore, the word "mystic" has an odious sound to some. But the mystics do not shut their mouths all the time and when they do speak, they provide information and harmony since their burning interest is communication both ways and their overriding feeling is love, which may become so strong that it wipes out hate, envy, pride, jealousy.

Some appreciate ancient mystics: Elijah, John the Baptist, St. Francis of Assisi, but shun the modern variety, such as Ralph Waldo Emerson, or the Turkish generals and statesmen, or Egyptian scholars, or RadnaKrishnan, India's philosopher and first President, or Dag Hammarskjold of United Nations fame, whom this writer knew from 1936 during his days in the Swedish Government.

By whatever name or method a mystic begins his trek, he ends up nameless, system-less, pride-less, self-less, seeing, hearing, feeling only one all-embracing Being whom, if he uses English terms, he may call God. He may begin as a Sufi, or a Yogi, or in one of the numerous organizations deriving from one of these, such as the Christian churches. Or he may begin all by himself, following no established path or creed.

As he fervently seeks to reach into the secrets of minerals, plants, animals, men, the universe, because he loves, because he wishes to be inside where he may understand, he can no longer stick to one creed, one name or one path not shared by everyone and everything. He does not deny. When with Christians, he tries to talk and behave as Christians do, as long as it is loving and not despising. When with Buddhists, he is a Buddhist, though not a judging one.

When with atheists, he assumes the fine flavor of the philosophical atheist who denies a primitive God but accepts a universal plan and planner. He enters the heart of every man and agrees with him; agrees with his deeper urges, not always with his superficial whims. And this is how he may appear to some as a teacher. He does not teach a doctrine. He only shows each person what this person himself deeply wishes. Many do not know what they deeply wish, so they may be shown by one who has learned to look deeper.

Where do we find this specimen called mystic? Everywhere, in every man and woman. A transparent example completed his life among us early in 1971. He left a thinly spread group, now increasing rapidly, in San Francisco and Marin County, polarized to him as teacher. They live in private homes or in community homes at all levels of comfort or discomfort. Many of them had been hippies and had taken drugs. Hardly any of them take drugs any more even though no one told them they had been wrong taking them. This they say, is due to this teacher, SAM or to their relation to him.

Samuel L. Lewis was a native San Franciscan and a horticulturist. Early he had an urge to find truth or at least, find something. The theories offered him in religion and science interested him but did not satisfy him. In 1910, an Eastern mystic, Inayat Khan, a Hindu musician of the Moinuddin Chishti order of Sufis, came to San Francisco. In 1923, Sam became his pupil. Though born of well-to-do parents, Sam's independence of spirit shaped for him a tough working-man's life and it was only in his seventies that he could afford to travel. To cover the greatest distance for the least funds, he relinquished all comfort and studied at the feet of many teachers, Buddhists, Hindus, Arabs, Japanese. He did not leave his old teachers as he acquired new ones, but coalesced them into a whole. One of his Sufi teachers in Pakistan dubbed him Sufi Ahmed Murad, meaning he who is endeavoring to fulfill his life's purpose, and when Sam's earth life had been completed, the same teacher redubbed him Sufi Ba Murad, meaning he who has accomplished his life's purpose.

Sam had already acquired a considerable following in San Francisco and each time he returned from his trips he threw himself into his work as teacher and organizer with renewed energy and a wider vision. One of his young pupils told me about the difference between Sam and another would-be teacher, a Zen Buddhist who incidentally was an old friend of Sam.

"And this Zen Buddhist travels all over the country lecturing to mass audiences telling them about the futility of talk, in line with Zen theory or idiosyncrasy, yet he talks and talks and that seems to be all he does, while Sam remains with me. He cares. This other fellow moves on and on to new audiences, new triumphs, forgetting the old ones, while Sam stays with me whether he is here or abroad. Sam is like my father, or brother, or son or, perhaps I should rather say, like myself, myself as I want to be. He knows when I am hungry and feeds me. He never argues, never criticizes or preaches. He's just there. I'm taking up my responsibilities in society again because of him, though he never told me to. He just has that confidence in me, more than I have myself. When I took those drugs I enjoyed the feeling of unity, I loved the weird visions but I lost my feeling of responsibility, I didn't care what I did or didn't do. I had no roots. Now I have roots and for the first time in my life I am enjoying them."

"You are working now?"

He flashed me a grimace, "I am trying to. I am applying in the fields I knew before all these things happened. The employers ask me uncomfortable questions. My past is all that seems to matter to them. Sam comes to my aid every time, telling them I am the finest in the world. So far that hasn't helped, except to keep up my self-respect."

"Missing the drugs?"

"No. With Sam I am enjoying all the same visions, and more of them, without the hangovers."

"How do you eat?"

"Sam has taken care of that. I'm a fixer and custodian in one of the community houses so my wife and I and our four-year-old eat well and proper every day, and feel as worthy of our keep as the other residents, most of whom work on the outside."

That same evening I watched Sam and a fragment of his crowd jubilate through a Shiva dance routine, accompanied by the rarest instruments from many corners of the world. Then Sam read a fiery manifesto, sparkling with wit and fury, from the then-leader of the Buddhist World Fellowship, Princess Poon Diskul of Thailand.

Suddenly Sam turned to me, "Pir-O-Murshid Inayat Khan just appeared to me telling me to share all my experiences with you."

Inayat Khan had been my teacher as well as Sam's. He had left this world forty years ago. Was Sam's remark just a friendly joke to an old fellow-pupil? To him it meant more. Was be right, then? Today practically nobody can tell. To assert one or the other version would be just plain superstition. For we have carelessly neglected certain promising and even essential aspects of living, searching and training, for generations. Sam, along with a few others, have at least taken steps to regain the lost kingdom.

The financial history of Sam's enterprises shows a gradual change. Some of the teachers Sam had met lived off gifts from their pupils. This is customary in the Far East but it was anathema to Sam in the beginning. He would rather give food and even clothing to his pupils, spending of his modest earnings. When later he inherited money, he spent it all on his crowd. Then businessmen among his pupils pointed out that this could not continue, there simply wasn't enough to run the enterprise this way. Sam went along and fees were set for entry into his classes and for instruction.

Sam's position and work were never a secret. Some say he shouted from the housetops. His contemporary, Dag Hammarskjold of the United Nations, on the other hand, kept his mystic trend hidden from all but a few trusted friends. Many hail this attitude as the essence of wisdom, and in view of Dag Hammarskjold's position, it might well have been. Sam's open door and un-secrecy may stem from a different kind of wisdom, from a different set of circumstances. For one thing, realizing, that if the mystic goods be not now openly sought and coveted, our civilization may face a dim future.

There is another difference between Sam and Dag. While the latter apparently had no specific individual teacher, Sam had many. Some mystics have claimed that you definitely need one teacher on this path. The Hindu mystic and poet Rabindranath Tagore in one of his stirring poems portrays the attainment of divine grace without the the assist of any teacher.

Who was right, Sam or Dag and Rabindranath?

All three were right. Sam wanted to know the world religions and teach them to others, so he needed to be taught. Rabindranath or the hero of his poem wanted to realize God, and who would insult our Creator by saying He is incapable of letting us know Him except through a go-between? The paths, streets and avenues are as many as there are human beings. Each one of us is unique, matchless, incomparable, in the final analysis his own one and only teacher.

The links to his various teachers made Sam international and historical. From the early Sufis, Abraham and, possibly, Chinese alchemists, there is a line of free and tolerant but disciplined thought and feeling down to such more recent teachers as Al Ghazali, who at the age of thirty-five reached fame as the outstanding scholar of both Christian and Moslem traditions. At that time, these two traditions might have merged. But, weary of the vagaries of fame, Al Ghazali left his sheltered world to roam as an unknown beggar. During his wanderings, he once came to a small town and entered a house of God to pray among the "little people". The preacher wound up his sermon praising "the great Al Ghazali, the top scriptural authority", not knowing that this famous man was in his audience.

Al Ghazali rose and quietly left, determined not to be trapped again in the web of fame.

Sam had much in common with Al Ghazali. He knew the Christian and Moslem traditions well and bridged them. In addition, he knew the Hindu and Buddhist traditions. In Sam's burning heart these were all one.

Late in his career, Sam learned to know and became deeply attached to Pir Vilayat, leader of the Sufi Order after his father Inayat Khan, Sam's first teacher, had passed away. I had known Pir Vilayat since he was ten years old, watched him gradually, courageously, ingeniously take on the burden of the mission his father had prepared him. A mystic in his own right, of unique clarity and beauty, a superb speaker and organizer, devoid of pose, of any sense of self, he reflects his father like the still waters of a lake on a windless night. And so does his brother Hidayat, whose music speaks to your soul.

Sam's friends and pupils lovingly followed and supported Pir Vilayat when their teacher Sam passed away.

Only a fraction of the mystic world has been touched here. One must enter and experience it to appreciate it. We read about Abraham, Ramakrishna, North, South, East, West. These persons or directions are bits and pieces without much sense before they are seen in relationship to each other and our own minds and hearts, as we seek and work toward TRUTH. You are an individual, original and unique, unlike any other, yet one with all, containing within you Abraham, Ramakrishna, North, South, East, West. You are one with all to such an extent that at moments you may know the other's thoughts, feelings, past and present as you know your own. You do not at first weigh these things in your mind or apply them, or accept or reject. You operate at first, in a medium beyond mind. There is no doubt, not even a mental recognition, just a factual knowledge, like you touch steel. You are happy, or rather beyond happiness. You are secure and realize this is the only security.

Now, when I try to garb these experiences in words, I have to let the mind play on them to paint an observable picture. I feel like cheating, I hope the viewer has seen at least part of it himself and so will be able to share and bear with me.

What I am trying to describe is not an imaginary state of mind. It is the same state that permitted Einstein to formulate his scientific outlook and may permit his successors to find and apply the equations Einstein sought but did not find. It is the state of mind that permits a financial wizard to see through the maze of money and accounting to the core of economics. It is the state of mind that permits a healer to see your ailment or his own, and correct it.

A prying Gallup Poll purported to find that ten per cent of us were mystics and had visions of one kind or another. Since most people are shy about gifts or blessings of this kind and would not reveal them to poll takers, may we conclude that most, or perhaps all of us, are genuine mystics?

What do rank-and-file mystics do? How do they spend their days? Michael and Benefsha spend many of them in Jerusalem, in tandem. While one is out there, bringing together Israelis, Arabs and Palestinians to work together, sing together, dance together, the other stays in San Francisco, keeping the home fires burning. They have no capital, travel on a shoe string, speak all languages. Michael, a horticulturist, builds greenhouses around Jerusalem, hoping thus to provide required capital. He also writes furious begging letters to friends and enemies, telling about living on cucumbers and yoghurt to make ends meet.

Some Arab youngsters recently rushed Benefsha in Jerusalem, inciting the crowd to lynch "the infidel". Benefsha is no infidel. She is a sufi, acknowledged by Hebrews, Christians and, particularly, by Muslims as the source and inspiration for all these religions. An old Arab sufi sheik sprang to her side. He had never seen her before, but sufis often recognize each other. He also knew Benefsha was so other-worldly, so devoted to her cause he could do anything physical to her without her even noticing. He pierced her neck with a sword, she told, her eyes widening, while he thundered to the young Arabs, "This is the proof what kind of person this girl is. Come forward, any one who thinks he is a better Arab than she, and we shall see!"

The youngsters fled before the old sheik could try his sword on them. Benefsha could continue her important work more safely than before. Such incidents pave the way toward peace in the Middle East.

WAR

The Nazi occupiers tried to force Norwegian youth to fight its Russian allies during World War II. They would have succeeded were it not that the Americans had kept their powder dry and threw out the Nazis. Worse, if Hitler had not been defeated by war, he would today have been running the world, based on nuclear power, and deciding where and for what every young man should fight and die. And some of my sincere, though ignorant American friends are appalled that I make my living building torpedoes, keeping America continuously prepared!

I was 44 when World War II started, considered too old to fight. I had to browbeat my way into the armed forces. In time, with British Intelligence and escaped German officers, we made detailed plans for kidnapping Hitler and ending the war early in 1944. The British were delighted. Franklin Roosevelt, at a safer distance from the front, turned us down, "The Germans must be beaten so they know it." If we, assigned to this mission, who had thus put our lives on the line, may be permitted a word, it is this: There are times when the horrors of war must be accepted to prevent greater horrors. I have met mutilated veterans and shuddered, "There, but for the grace of God, go I," but even these tell me they would have done it again.

In addition, the nation's economy ran smoother, the living standard soared and somber warnings that we would be ruined in the future came to naught, for the sacred goal of winning welded us into efficient working units so we put out ample goodies in addition to munitions. We were close together. All talents were sought and used. We did not waste away our lives in unemployment. While some of us fought on the outside, the nation's insides were warm, healthy and compassionate.

This reminded us that we had been unable in peace time to grasp the urgent needs that ought to have kept us all as busy as the more obvious need of winning a war.

The smoothly running economy made the war look attractive, to the non-combatants at least, with the consequence that World War II, for example, was prolonged far beyond its useful life. This writer was involved, as a linguist, soldier and adventurer, in the first German approaches to Allied quarters. The war was not old when high-placed Germans offered to help dispose of the Hitler gang and establish a new cooperative German government. There was every reason to believe in their sincerity, as well as their ability to carry out their plans. Never more than forty-four per cent of the German people had ever voted for Hitler; most years much less. He had beaten and murdered his way to power in spite of the fifty six per cent or most who opposed him. He never represented the German people.

Among those who favored the plans of the German dissidents were Allan Dulles, at that time only a minor U.S. intelligence operator who could not yet swing the minds of Premiers and Presidents; Trevor Roper, British historian and intelligence operator, and others in the thick of action though thin in power. Platitudes, such as "We must beat the Germans so they know it," were countered by British General J. F. Fuller, "The fifty-six percent majority of Germans don't need that lesson. The rest cannot be taught and do not matter."

Greater names had their way, ignoring General Fuller, and have weighing on their conscience (if such exists after death?), millions of American, British and continental lives, among which the very Germans who could make the post-war years worthy of the sacrifices.

What, in the scheme of things, caused the emergence of a Hitler gang and its wars? A short-circuit in the current that feels and knows that every living being represents the universe. Hitler, near-sighted, fancied his limited person and his friends represented it against others who did not. But how could this unholy mixture of imagination, lies and hypocricies be accepted by such a substantial part of a great people? Because of intolerable pressure brought about by clumsy, inoperable economic sanctions. Once launched, Hitler's thrusts at first were more successful than even he had expected, for none of his powerful neighbors lifted a hand to defend the victims. Atrocious crimes were committed against people and races while the world sat still in the name of PEACE, which from then on became a dirty word and still may be.

One by one, we finally awoke and saw that there was something greater than peace, morally and practically greater and more necessary. That morally and practically greater thing was WAR.

We learned that war itself is neither wrong nor necessarily right. What is wrong is that we start wars too late and carry them on too long.

The Korean war, predictable to the wary, came as an unpleasant surprise to those American leaders who had sent Phillip Jessup, a distinguished John Hopkins scholar, to East Asia, ostensibly on a "fact-finding" mission. Equally distinguished foreign service officers had collected facts for centuries in those same areas, so nobody swallowed this version of the mission. I happened to be on a lower level, partly self-inflicted mission in the same area at this same time and the pretensions of Jessup's mission so galled me that I deposited with a friend in the Embassy of Tokyo, a less than scholarly treatise on the subject of FACTS, postulating that in international relations, particularly, facts are not "found" but made. Dr. Jessup is rumoured to have chuckled over it.

So, we waited for the real purpose of Jessup's visit to be revealed. It was. In the first spot of his landing, and thereafter in every following place, he said, with variations, that Asia must not expect from the United States a participation or an aid program in any way comparable to our European commitments. This was Dr. Jessup's mission: Not to find a fact but to produce one. What he produced was the Korean war. This may not have been his explicit purpose, nor the purpose of those who sent him. But our distinguished North Korean, Chinese and Russian counterparts interpreted to the best of their ability these statements, then staged the invasion of South Korea on the apparently well-founded belief that the United States would not interfere.

My own appearance in Japan at Christmas 1949 was not solely to take part in General MacArthur's perennial New Year Party at the Imperial Hotel, although this was worth the trip all by itself for you were permitted and even urged to hug and kiss the entire complement of American womanhood in the area from age eighty down to sixteen, at midnight sharp, and the Geishas to boot. In addition, I had been commissioned by a friend to retrieve about a hundred thousand dollars worth of gold dust deposited by a fugitive from the Bolsheviks near Blagovaschensk on the river Amur. My friend had also involved U.S. intelligence. This project held no treasure hunt charm for me; for if I survived at all there would be nothing left for me after the Russians had taken their share and my friend what he considered his. But it was as good an excuse as any for going in and seeing what the Russkies were up to . . . a fact-finding mission after all?

How far up the MacArthur hierarchy my plan was supported I do not know, but with the ranks it was a shoe-in. All information that could be obtained was badly needed. But the local representative of the State Department said no, and so probably saved my life, though was it worth saving?

So the Korean war came along without my assistance. It took thousands of American and Korean lives to prove that America, as a whole, did not share the sentiments of those appointed officials who sent Dr. Jessup on his fact-producing mission. The United States, a giant rider straddling Europe and Asia, can never ignore the plight of either.

My Tokyo friends told me that while I could not enter the Soviet Union from Japan, there was no objection to my entering from any other point. So, I had the most cordial encounter with Ivanshenko in Hong Kong, officially Russian Trade Commissioner, actually one of the eminences behind the vast and secret Russian gold. He told me a hundred thousand dollars worth was like a grain of sand compared to Russia's actual holdings. But this grain of sand, I countered, might nevertheless become of some interest to certain Russians and Americans? Seeing Ivanshenko's cold stare. I quickly emptied my glass of vodka and sank deeply into the armchair trying to become invisible.

I made a daring thrust as far as Chungking, China's ancient capital, where I happened to see Chiang Kai-Shek, long since rumored to be in Taiwan, standing very erect in a luxurious overcoat, back-slapping and well-wishing his associates, then emplaning for Taiwan; an insouciant, unworried target for red snipers. Whatever his politics, the old man displayed regal courage.

Further penetration became impossible. Reluctantly I had to backtrack, using the last exiting missionary plane, the St. Paul, outrageously overloaded, a pile of furniture and trunks in the middle of the floor upon which the children played mountaineers, yelling their WHOOPEES while the missionaries prayed earnestly that the plane would lift, which it did, obligingly, knocking two telephone poles in the noble effort.

The Korean war brought us in close touch with long-term torture as a government policy. A village chief not yet proven, merely being suspected of being anti-red friend-of-yanks would be strung up and slowly tortured through weeks. His dead body would continue to hang there until the stink would duly have impressed upon all what happens if you don't play ball. Many of our boys seeing this, fought more fiercely, hoping to produce a impression of their own. But some worried whether this zeal might be exposed to the same kind of torture, which might eat away their enthusiasm. There was another creeping fear: That our troops might become brutalized infected with this same disregard for fellow-humans. This, in addition to strategic and tactical reasons, was why all our military men became convinced we must never again become involved in a land war in Asia. General Ridgeway, who knew the ins and outs of the Korean war was a major spokesman for this view, along with Genera Gavin. If the so-called "military mind" could have prevailed, we might not have been in Vietnam at all, even though visible and invisible pressure from less knowledgeable Presidents and their entourages caused many officers to condone our land war in Vietnam.

The "military mind" syndrome was indulged in even by such

an intellect as Jawaharlal Nehru. He used the expression when we talked about President Eisenhower. Later, when he had seen and talked to him, he admitted he had been mistaken. "I have never met a man more genuinely concerned with peace." A military man, with experience in his ghoulish line, knows the horrors of war and that all means must be employed to avoid it.

As for myself, hailing from Norway, which has not been attacked since the Atlantic Pact was signed because, I believe, the U.S. dropped hints it would go to war if Norway was invaded - I wondered if the Korean war would have happened at all if the U.S. instead of shouting that Asia would have to take care of itself, had said, as in the case of Norway, that an attack would be squarely met.

In Asia, in addition, there is China. What do we know of China? More than anyone else in the Western World. Apart from all our immigrants from China and citizens of Chinese descent, the U.S. has more people who know and understand China than any other nation. Through such people, the Mainland Chinese government has made probings through the years. Forced by an irate section of the citizenry, our government has remained aloof and non-committal until now, finally, there has been a coming-together.

The priceless benefit of the Vietnam war has been the revelation it provided of our volatile emotions and stunted thought patterns, upon which might possibly follow a sobering process. Here an oversized half of the nation pompously proclaimed that all we did was thoughtlessly intrude into a domestic quarrel at a fabulous price in lives and billions. The undersized rest of us thought we had honestly tried to save a striving democracy from cruel and reactionary red bullies.

The former say: Who could connect the term "bully" with good old Ho Chi Minh's saintly face with the long, silky beard? My French friends told me he sold his own commie friends (those he didn't like) to the French secret police and their torture chambers. Senior Congressperson Frances Bolton asked me in the sixties what to do about requests for vast increases in our troops to Vietnam. I said I would love to have helped my South Vietnamese friends - possibly by some intelligence action or naval operations; but more land forces in Vietnam would not help, would destroy more than we could build. I have compassion for my countrymen who had to make those fateful decisions, though I wonder why they did not listen to senior Generals Ridgeway and Gavin, the misunderstood and abused "military minds".

We might have "won" in Vietnam, by conducting the war on military principles rather than as a parlor game, but what would be the sense of destroying a country and its future livability just because a cruel band had ruled and mistreated its citizens and threatened others? No secure haven would have been created, just wastelands, more hate and additional blood baths.

All this we learned in or from Vietnam, though at a price. Some of us, who found the facts too hard to face, took refuge in drugs. This was also correctly foreseen by our so unappreciated "military minds" who are now busy controlling and reversing this trend, incidentally just a fraction of the nation's alcohol problem.

While hardly a word has been heard in this country about Ho Chi Minh, this former CIA hireling, and what he has cost our country in lives and billions, former President Thieu of South Vietnam who headed a government of our own creation, has been continuously misrepresented and mistreated by "important", ignorant and infantile writers. May we learn from this?

War is destruction, though occasionally it fosters greatness. Muclus Scaevola, a Roman patriot, volunteered to kill Lars Porsena who was besieging Rome, just like modern CIA agents today volunteer to risk death and torture to protect us. Mucius was caught and sentenced to be burned alive. Smilingly, he placed his right hand into a coal fire until it was burned to a crisp. This is why he was later called Scaevola, the lefthanded one. Lars was so impressed, he freed Mucius and gave up the siege.

In Norway, during the Nazi occupation, I met men who had been repeatedly tortured, in a way few ever survived, to make them reveal names of the underground. They were treated to boiling enemas that seemed to burn out their insides.

"How can you stand it?"

"There comes a time when you don't care any longer what happens to you. You know only one thing: You are not going to give."

"What about the pain?"

"The pain I first felt was half fear, fear of death. I don't fear death any more, so I feel only half the pain. It is bearable."

Such sentiment may not make sense to one who is thrown into a war he does not understand or can't believe in. But a volunteer who knows he defends his country, his ideal, sees such moments as pinnacles of achievement. They are. To him, war lifts him above his human limitations to touch his Creator.

The many more, whom war does not lift, to whom war is unacceptable cruelty, what hope can they be given? No promise of eternal peace, only the prospect that through diligent study of man in all parts of the world, we may reach an insight that will permit us to diminish causes of major wars and eventually substitute police functions.

First of all, our present volatile "deterrent" system can be changed. One contemplated alternative was presented in *Foreign Affairs*, January 1973, by Fred Charles Ikle, former professor of political science at MIT and recently closely connected with weapons systems and strategy.

Dr. Ikle hopes to eliminate the vulnerability of our strategic arms to surprise attack and thus break the vicious circles: That they must be ready for prompt launching because they are vulnerable, and they are vulnerable because they must be ready. Weapons incapable of quick launching are less suitable for surprise; and against truly invulnerable nuclear armaments, surprise would have lost its purpose. For example, he proposes, arms hidden deeply underground, which could be launched only through weeks or months, would permit second thoughts, change of mind when warranted, over-riding panic decisions or correcting faulty messages. This, he admits, seems like a small step, but may be a beginning that might well save this globe from destruction.

Careful techno-socio-psychologic studies must precede such a step. Is it not possible, for example, that an enemy knowing it would take weeks or months before retaliation could strike would go ahead with his attack, believing he could counter the counter attack by some means when given that much time? And might he not be right? An adventurous or even erratic bossman might well gamble. But the idea is worth serious consideration.

Now the sixty-nine billion dollar question: What causes wars? As for World War II, the answer was easy: Hitler. But why did such a character gain power in Germany? What level of despair caused a great people to listen to his ravings?

The German economy was out-of-kilter. Germans starved. The payments imposed on Germany after World War I were to be made, not in German goods exported to the Allies - the only way in which any nation can pay. No, the payments were to be made in dollars and other non-German currency. How could Germany obtain dollars? Only by selling German goods in the States. But we refused to let them do that. We were afraid this would increase our own unemployment. We tried, like other Western nations, to maintain what we called a "favorable" trade balance, meaning to sell for more than we bought. The only way any one can maintain such a "favorable" balance is for others to have an unfavorable one. On this self-destructing principle has the world economy operated - or misoperated, and still does.

For many years now thoughtful people have shown us how continuous full employment could be achieved, with the greatest benefit to our national economy, to our freedoms, and to our trade balance. That's what this book is all about, particularly our concluding chapter. So, if not directly, then indirectly one major cause of World War II was the chaotic national economics. In other words: That full employment as national policies had not been established.

Today we have nuclear arms. A war will be more deadly. We have a choice between full employment or destruction.

Riots: A Challenge?

Science has the healthy habit of reversing itself before it becomes stale. For some time now, psychiatry has told us crowding caused violence and since crowding was obviously increasing, violence was too - a good alibi for doing nothing. Then some doubters took a look at London, Tokyo, Holland, where people live in a more crowded condition than anywhere in the U.S. or than they ever did before; yet, in these places violence is at a minimum and, will you believe it? Decreasing!

So we have a chance for improvement, but how? If you look closely at a rioting crowd, it becomes no longer just "a crowd". Well at the back you notice thoughtful, often well-groomed planners who move cautiously so they won't get hurt, or dirtied. Well up front are some whose impulses have been shifted from their minds to arms, legs, fists and mouths. They run, throw, hit, kick and shout from sheer lust. The rest, without whom the planners and the kickers would mean nothing and could not act, are those who have been humbled, trodden upon and so neglected that they are now willing to trade pain for gain, even if it be others' gain. To these we owe, not alms, but answers.

What answers? More police? Longer jail terms? That might lead to less riots today; certainly more and worse riots tomorrow. Then what about substituting medical care for jail? Catalyzers? Psychiatry? That wouldn't help either, in the long run, unless. . .

Unless something else is done, too - something that does not cost us money but which earns us money.

A person usually earns money as he produces. Everybody knows that. Few think of it in the terms of the whole nation, and it is even more true of a nation. The nation as a whole earns more as more people join in production, if management is at the United States level. Since not all people are busy producing now, we have less money around, a lower living standard than we could and should have. Besides, we now produce a few things nobody wants. While production creates money, some of this money is cancelled again when products don't sell. Any new production must be geared to what is wanted, needed.

Who hasn't heard about market analysis? Any good business finds out in advance what people want by asking questions in surveys. What we need now is a market analysis not merely of the old-timers in the field of gadgets, clothes or cars, but a real comprehensive survey of what people want if all the new exciting things science has brought out should be produced and marketed. To some small extent, this is going on all the time but until manufacturers scream for any-and-all living, two-legged humans to work and produce for them, we aren't doing enough.

Our versatile computers - what we now have and new creations - are just raring to go and determine, with and for us, what manpower and organizing talent is available or can be made available to produce what we need or want, and bring every one into the stream of things. Some of our largest firms, particularly in the aerospace field, have dipped into "unemployables" as they were termed during our superstitious early sixties. We have found that they are not only employable but sometimes better, more steady than the current average.

However, the prospect of a much higher living standard does not come from the additional employment, but from the yet-unused resources of science. Recently developed scientific products, methods, computers, services may boost our living standard substantially in desired directions if we put our minds to it, if we decide to develop these vast potentials. The ensuing affluence will make it easy to employ all, regardless of their so-called "efficiency", and offer to all a dignified living.

Americans working abroad who, for example, trained Hindu and Vietnamese peasants to become plumbers and mechanics never believed in the "unemployable" dogma. They know a little about how to train a person "from scratch" and, not the least, how good such people are apt to become; faster than you could imagine. Firms and government agencies working "in the ghettoes" might do well seeking out these experienced Americans who now sit around in insignificant jobs underemployed. There is little reason why Americans should copy the folly of the British who nurtured two nations within their little island: The proud, narrow homebodies, retaining all power, and the much-knowing, but so humble travelers, so well-mannered nobody paid them heed.

When we decide to act, to provide a national economy to absorb any and all willing to work - then and then only have we a clear case. After that, we may calmly crush any effort at rioting. Then, it will be our duty. Then, we need no more reminders.

If we do not take any such clear and decisive step, there will be bigger and bloodier riots whatever else we try to do to stop them.

Our riots are reminders and warnings to take stock of our assets, potentialities. Especially, they are warnings to the nation's managers and leaders: Are we managing well?

The fashion today is to gather praise from all over the world about American business management. In the limited task of managing an established business with a set crew according to rigid rules and extensive note-taking, report-writing and filing, the American management systems are fair. Entirely different systems are required for expanding employment gradually to all. Flexibility, brains and manners are required; above all: heart. Will the exec team as a whole listen and learn from those who tried?

If riots are reminders, particularly to management, to management in private industry, in government, in communications, business - then who is doing the reminding? And why? Are there other reminders? Maybe a whole slew of them?

May we try to look at the things happening in life from a point of view other than our own? To us many happenings appear bothersome, insulting; punches in the nose. But suppose we think up a hypothetical "something" planning men's lives? This "something" may not necessarily be outside ourselves, but rather a collective subconscious or superconscious of which we already have so many indications that several branches of science have begun to hypothesize and even research. Such common gadgets as automobiles are being looked upon not merely as means of transportation but as instruments for developing men's character. If for one second he does not keep his attention focused, he may die! Could there be a better stimulus to alertness, keenness, consideration?

The airplane was invented and launched. It required attention of a different kind, and a thoughtful mind. Space became a profession to the deep thinker in symbols, the mathematician and the quick, attentive astronaut. Man branched into many avenues of high accuracy, punctual attention to requirements of a complex nature.

If such a planning supermind actually exists, we begin now to guess his purpose: Could it be building, checking and testing mind and personality?

Personality?

Well, suppose that this planning agency placed fortunates and unfortunates, haves and have-nots - rather close to each other, practically as neighbors, just to evoke mutual interest and compassion? But suppose that the placing them near each other did not help much, that the fortunates showed little interest; indeed tried to shut their eyes and put cotton in their ears so they would not see or hear what, to them, seemed unpleasant? Then, obviously, this planning agency, drawing from all the people, not merely from the few here considered, would have to resort to more dramatic events that could not fail to impress - riots?

What? Do I mean to imply that riots really come from ourselves? From a mysteriously expanded multimind? Who knows? As I look and feel and check, more and more things and happenings seem to fall within the category of semi-mysterious planning - though much of this planning may be in the area of statistical mathematics. This means that not every single detail seems to be planned or, in other words, appears to be operating according to established law, but the general trend is or does.

In nuclear physics, statistical mathematics blazed the trail to most of the solutions. So why not in the relationship between citizens, between the fortunates and the unfortunates, between the haves and have-nots?

Statistical mathematics demonstrate that:

"As we sow, so shall we reap" in a general way. As we are curious, so shall we know. As we know, so, accordingly, shall we act.

And, vice-versa: If we put cotton in our ears (well, in our mental ears!) and if we cover our eyes, if we refuse to hear and refuse to see, then we shall reap - riots. Little reminders.

But why? Laws have just been passed that guarantee so many rights, so many privileges. . . Yes, laws have been passed but how many have gained satisfactory employment? How many have begun to feel they are useful, needed? How many have begun to eat right? To laugh right? To walk with a bouncing step?

Statistical mathematics, through the best of its equations, works out the answers from the facts. Statistical mathematics does not lie much. Statistical mathematics may be a planner's tool.

And riots are among its props.

The French Revolution - "Liberty, Equality, Brotherhood" - provides a forceful lesson - a two-edged warning, both to those who launch riots and to those who suffer them, without taking action.

Two men were fighting for power in France: King Louis XVI and the merchant, Jacques Necker. Jacques Turgot, Louis' Finance Minister, and friend Ben Franklin fed lines to the King from the prompter's box. Franklin kept in close touch with the French ever since his term as "Minister Plenipotentiary" to France, from 1779 to 1785. Louis XVI, unlike his great-great-grandfather Louis XIV, was a man of ideals and ideas and had the public welfare in mind. Necker was a grain merchant. He alternatively withheld grain, or flooded the market, making a fortune on people's hunger. He extended his operations to other areas, became a master of finance and offered large loans to the Crown, wanting to become the "power behind the throne".

The King, supported by his Finance Minister, refused the offer and coined his own government money. Necker responded by crying "Inflation!" in his many newspapers, then touched his financial buttons to produce it.

Louis, seeing through the scheme, confined Necker to his lavish home from where the shrewd financier continued his influence through prepared channels. He hired professional rioters to move on the Palace.

Here is where both parties came to grief. The professionals were joined by such a horde of malcontents - who did not know what, where, how - that the leadership lost control. The revolution for freedom and equality was launched. The emerging "brotherhood" swallowed and destroyed both combatants and set the nation back to a dark age of cruelty, disease and debilitation.

Such is the end result of successful rioting.

Love, How Real?

Was there ever a word more awkward to define? And, for that very reason, more thrillingly divine? Above all, what has it to do with dreary economics? Histrionics? Half or full employment? Matrimonics? Flushing your veins with a scent of spring or with the majestic glow of fall and causing the Heavenly bodies to dance in space, it is called by many names.

To the unwary youth, it is sex; to the blushing maiden, her heart; to the artist, his dream; to the scientist, his every try; to the musician, his tune-in; and to the God-seeking: GOD.

The maddest of all is the last one: The seeker and lover of GOD. Swathed in his fantasia robe he sees all following his path. Whatever they begin to love, they will end up - he knows - loving only that one and final ALL, that one and only Being - GOD.

He sees the sex-bitten, first walking like a drunk, flailing, wildly, helplessly, his only aim being to thoroughly possess the beloved. In the course of this quest, which the drunkard first thinks of as a conquest, he discovers there is no satisfaction without consent; there is no happiness without communication, understanding. He is no drunkard any longer. Urgent interest chimes forth; feverish curiosity in all aspects of the beloved - body, mind, heart, aspirations. So, from sex springs love.

With the glow of understanding of the beloved, understanding of one human being other than himself, more and more follow; interest in all follows. Interest in and understanding of other nations follows. "International relations" become two words with meaning. The real and genuine profit, however, is that with understanding people, he obtains a glimpse of that many-splendored SOME-

THING that made the people. He looks at and understands people: Actually he looks at and understands GOD through His windows that are the people.

Ah, to such a seer, to such an observer come many thrills; through and beyond the apparent faults and shortcomings he sees the pattern. The goal toward which shortcomings and assets, sins and virtues alike - are stepping stones. Rungs in the ladder up which he climbs!

"What is wrong with the world" are not words of a seer. They are words of the blind.

"What is right with the world" are the corresponding words of the seer, the lover.

Love, when you get down to analyzing it, turns out to be, not an emotion, nothing that vague - but a realization.

Realization of what?

Realization of the togetherness of us creatures. Looking at our physical bodies, we look very much separated. Looking deeply into our minds, we see that we hang together like the branches of a tree. And who or what is the stem?

Guess, won't you?

As you grow, with time, you may look back, occasionally, at your discarded idea that we are separate beings, and it begins more and more to look like a side-splitting joke - until you notice the tragic consequences of this superstition. Then you don't laugh any more, for although the solution appears to be near and clear to you it is unattainable at the present time. It is unattainable, not for lack of intelligence. The ocean of intelligence is here, common to all, available to all, always open, always ready to be poured from.

The lack is of another kind: Lack of love. Perhaps one should rather say: Lack of discovery of love. For love is there too, a frothing, surging stream. It just has to be discovered, then tapped. Love is the driving force that harnesses and uses will, intelligence, muscle.

How may this surging stream of love be discovered? Ask the lovers. They have difficulty not finding it, but restraining it. So they may eat and live on. Most of our lovers are so blinded by their particular object of love that they know practically nothing of love itself - the stream. Through disappointments and sufferings, they may learn if they have the guts to learn.

The first love of the arriving soul is the mother and a little later, the father. This first love of the baby and child for its parents is delightfully intertwined with hunger, greed and all those little things we blandly term selfishness. This term is involved in all of life and it isn't as bad as rumored.

Suppose one or both parents are unworthy of the child's love and cannot evoke it? This is a matter for concern but not worry. Countless children have jumped the gap to more mature and deeper love for a mate or child or teacher later in life, so that the difficulty with the parents became a spur to depth and clarity. Others did not seem able to pull themselves out of the hole parental negligence dug. Community care, county-state and-federal, have an opportunity here. The greater opportunity is that of friends.

The dating and mating season is much more difficult. Casualties abound. All your resources come into play here: The tenure and texture of your love, its depth, your judgement your self-control, your resolve. With minor wounds, most players emerge in a fair enough condition to submit to the grueling try-out of married life. Could even the keenest planner have devised a more telling test.

Nobody can endure married life except through a love so deep that it forgets selfish urges in the effort to please the beloved. This is how LOVE is discovered.

Not everybody is tailored to this particular type of love or even if they are, it may not happen to them. To some, their principal love is their profession, their work, their science - or their religion. They may be unmarried or, again, they may be just as happily married as anybody else, but their marriage may be bent to a more demanding love. A wise wife, even if she does not directly share her husband's work or ideal, will readily submit and by so doing evoke a love in her husband that he was not capable of before. An unwise wife will nag - or divorce.

From the early days in school through the University and on through the laboratories, the working places - and the churches - there is another object of love: The teacher.

This often is a very pure and deep love that is closer than any other form to the essence of love. Intertwined with the personal admiration are the inspiration, the logic, the thrilling contents of a profession, a trade, a religion.

Is it proper to mention the trade, the profession, the science and the work in the same breath as religion?

Yes, all are from the Great Creator; all are designed for the education and development of man. In the good old days, the professions and the work were not so varied. The bearing of these aspects of life upon the essence was not so fully realized. Therefore, in the ancient traditions one hears so much about religion, so little about these other things, these other paths, these other aspects of religion. One might say that all of them were embodied in the beautiful symbology of the religious traditions.

To a great many people, religion has something beyond and above these other aspects. While a school teacher or an advanced scientist may be equated with a minister or rabbi, a Hodja or a priest, religion, in addition, has the prophet, the Savior, the founder, the "Son of God" (we are all sons or daughters of God but some are more consciously so). In religion there is the great master, the Perfect One to some, the best One to others, who will embrace you in a life-giving, everlasting stream of love if you accept Him. This is a climax, though it is not the final climax. In your adoration of the Master you try to be like him. That is essential. It is not enough to adore him or love him. Well, it is enough for some - for the time being. But in some phase of life you will have to go further - to become like that master; in a sense to BECOME THAT MASTER. That is why the Master said, "There is no path to God except through me." Every Master has said the equivalent. It means that through the loving example you reach that love that reveals GOD.

Today, some scientists replace in many people's mind the Master of religion and that is quite all right. Each one can and should follow only the ideal he finds in his heart. He finds it in his heart after having perused books or lectures. He finds it there because his heart so responds.

Some people arrive at a love of GOD without having gone

through the love of a man, a teacher, a MASTER, a Prophet. They deserve as much respect, as much admiration, as much recognition as those who took the road via a Master - perhaps even more, in some cases - who knows? Who is there to pronounce judgment?

The proof is in the pudding: Has such a direct God-lover become of more service to his fellowmen, or less, or just as much, as those other travellers? Beware, even before you pronounce a verdict on this latter issue!

Whether the path goes through the Prophet or directly, it is glittering, gleaming with the gold of a love sweeter, mightier, more genuine than the love of a mother, a wife, a friend, the best teacher.

In the cycle of a human life, there is a love more compassionate, more selfless and more pure than that of a child for his parent or, usually, that of a mate for the other mate. That is the love of a parent for his child. This is why God is often pictured as the Father or, in India for example, as a Mother, too. The love of God could not have been better expressed in the language of men than by the love of a Father or Mother.

A person may reach that blessed stage of parental love for his children after he has experienced all other facets of love including the love of a teacher, the love of a humanized Lord, Master, Messiah, Savior, Son of God! He will then love his children with wideness and depth and with a fiber woven from all these stirring facets of love and life.

A person may go through the human cycle of love only, without the addition of the love of profession or religion, and still reach a stirring and deep love for his children, a love that will filter down as blessings to his children and their childrens' children - for all aspects of Love are but one: The stream of love through and by which this universe with all its beings was created and is being maintained.

Therefore, love is the basis for a society and its economics. If love abounds, society flourishes. If love ebbs, there is danger of dissolution.

I am Just an Accident

I am just an accident, said Ralph. He was a biologist with a brilliant career behind him and, possibly, an even more brilliant one ahead. His new strains in grain, his Chlorella research had caused our anxious forecasts in the sixties about a coming mass starvation in the mid-seventies to be reversed into worries about how to get rid of huge food surpluses in the seventies.

"That. too, was just an accident," insisted Ralph, "and a temporary one. Over the long haul, there will be shortages, starvation."

There was a chill in his voice. You wondered: Bitterness? Cynicism? Or just light banter? Obviously, Ralph was not a happy man, though you couldn't pin him down. He was always on the move. If bitter today, he might be bitter-sweet tomorrow, semi-sweet the day after.

Opposite him sat Fred, an astrophysicist who, like most physicists, enjoyed playing mind games.

"If you and I are accidents, Ralph, then so is the whole wide world. Is this a cause for humility - or pride?"

Fred had known Ralph as long as he could remember and played the role of comforter or teaser. He saw in his friend a whimsical archetype who passed through all the stages of human development represented in history, not just once but again and again, in rapid repetition. This, held Fred, was the pattern for academia in modern America. No rest. Constantly on the way, up or down. A product of the deductive educational process.

"The insects might have won, you know," said Ralph. "By a mere accident, the ants lost out."

"And you are sorry?"

"I sometimes worry whether the ants would have done a better job, with their togetherness, their discipline. Maybe they would have been more deserving of inheriting the Earth."

"You are a biologist. Have you seen how the ants punish the undisciplined?"

"They kill them. While among us, the disciplined are being killed by the undisciplined."

"We grant life to our protesters."

"And let them murder us."

"Not all of us, Ralph. You and I are still around."

"So we are, Fred, so we are. But 10,000 of us will be murdered this year says Don Lunde of Stanford. More of us were murdered between 1970 and 74 than were killed through the entire Vietnam war. We have a murder epidemic in this country now. Twice as many are put away now than twenty years ago."

"And why? Professor Lunse sees the reason in the vast number of unemployed. I feel in my bones he is right. If I were given the boot, and thought I would never again work, never again see a pay check - as the unemployed always fancy - I'd feel like murdering a few people too."

"You defend those murderers?"

"Silly! I think they are almost as bad as we are, when we condemn to death and then cold-bloodedly murder defenseless prisoners, after we first have insulted them."

"Almost as bad? You mean when we, supported by law, execute criminals, we are worse than murderers?"

"A little worse, yes, in that we do it even without passion and without the slightest risk to ourselves, We need not even see the guy, or the gruesome procedure. What is worse: We do not really know if he has done what we say he has done."

"He will have been duly tried, won't he?"

"And so? In law we have something called circumstantial evidence. It means that with our faulty human reasoning some of us say this person is guilty while others, every bit as able, say he is not. We call this "justice". So isn't killing through "law" just a bit worse than an average murder?"

"What would you do, Fred?"

"First of all, employment for every willing hand, all his life, without interruption, at wages that will keep goodies running as required or desired and keep money fairly stable. . ."

"A tall order, Fred."

"No, Ralph. It is a less tall order than what you do as a matter of course in your laboratory, and which later is being repeated in the factories. We all tend our little store and pay no attention to our common employment and economy situation, which is well within the power of Americans to manage."

Ralph has gone a long way since this trifling dialogue. He still feels he may be just an accident, but this no longer bothers him. He still remembers that the insects might have won, but far from worrying about that, he now tries to make the best of man's "accidental" victory.

Sounds easy? It took a lot of doing! There was his career and his wife. He loved both, and both gave him trouble. He loved his wife with a passion as well as a tender depth. He wanted so much to please her, to satisfy her. His wish was blazened by his passion into a raging storm. The raging storm blew his mind into every part of her mind and heart and, like little searchlights, these bits of his mind picked up her messages and then he knew her, knew what she was, what she wanted, knew it without knowing that he knew. So he pleased her and he satisfied her.

His original theories in biology were not believed by his associates, so he had to invent and carry out a broad, comprehensive set of tests through which he found, not his original theories, but something much wider and better. He also found the recognition of his erstwhile detractors.

His mind and heart had now become accustomed to deep, even passionate probings. As he had probed his wife, so he probed the minds and attitudes of his friends and colleagues. He learned to know them, know their secrets. He pleased them and satisfied them.

He did not stop there. He began to wonder about life then, wonder why his mind had that power to probe and search-and find. It seemed like a miracle. It seemed so because everything and anything a man does not understand, he calls a miracle. Then, if he is a scientist he is not permitted to accept miracles. He must reject what he cannot explain.

Ralph had learned not to reject. First, he tried to understand. What he could not understand or explain, he shoved into a spacious attic in his mind marked "judgment suspended". He did not want to emulate Vannevar Bush, called America's greatest scientist at the time when he proclaimed that jet engines had no future, either in military or civilian aviation. The very adjective "great" made Ralph shudder. Einstein had come and gone and still scientists pretended to look at a world outside them and independent of them, and measure it. They still failed to see that they existed in and with this world, never apart from it, and could only measure their own individual relation to it. The apparent identical trend in some of our simple everyday experiences deceive the unwary.

Biologist Ralph, concerned with the feeding and survival of his species, was conducting a crash-study of chlorella, a highly nutritious algae, and his path crossed the Chinese who had brought this art further along than anybody else. Born and raised in what has been called a WASP environment: White, Anglo-Saxon, Protestant; Ralph wondered and marveled at the Chinese attitude toward life, termed synchronistic by Western psychiatrist Carl Jung, as contrasted to the Western causal concept. Dr. Jung elaborates, saying the Chinese look at and accept the world and life in their natural state, with all the complexities, and try to unravel the riddles from there, while the West tries to reason all and everything into a system of cause and effect. "Actually they can do that only in artificial laboratories where certain factors have been removed in order to obtain confirmation of the 'natural laws' we imagine we have 'discovered'." Dr. Jung goes on to say that many physicists of the West now appear to have embraced a synchronistic rather than a causal concept.

Ralph also noticed a difference in languages. The Western languages he knew were built on opposites: Good-evil, black-white, clean-dirty, strong-weak, while the Chinese languages, and particularly Mandarin, evaded such sharp contrasts, as if those speaking these languages were more polite and also more accurate observers who saw the fine shades.

His get-together with the Chinese became a turning point in Ralph's life. He had learnt to know the people most different from his own. He used to say that the Chinese had become for him his passport to humanity and, he added, to the Creator of humanity. Where could you see the Creator except through his creatures?

This was a startling and somewhat embarrassing discovery, for this Creator of the Chinese would then obviously also be the creator of himself, of his body, mind, heart, soul - whatever soul was. So he, Ralph, with accoutrements, was made by the same Creator and was just as important as any Chinese, including the *First?*

While Ralph has made this exciting trip from a crude and hazardous view of himself, society and the ants to a substantial though still tentative self-respect, others are fuming: What does such finery matter when we are going to starve to death from overpopulation anyway?

Are we? Yes, if we wish to, though of food and energy sources there is no end in sight, except to those who insist on seeing only one type. From Melbourne, Australia, comes a relevant book on *Practical Statistics* (and its follies) by Russell Langley. His first chapter is about false percentages, fictitious precision, misleading presentations, incomplete data, faulty comparisons - all daily ingredients in our news menus, tending to hide the recent changes in the food picture: New strains, new sources, and the resolution into regional differences of our once apparently unchangeable population trends and policies. In some areas, the rise in population was drastically curtailed unassisted by any drive, such as in the United States. Other countries have empty areas to fill, economic goals to reach that require increased population rise, such as Brazil, Bolivia, Kenya, Tunisia. In the latter country this author had some experience, heading a United Nations Mission.

Dr. Karl Brandt, former Director of Stanford University's Food Research Institute and former Presidential Science Advisor, has written continuously about this, long before it became popular, and recently sighed, "I feel like writing a book, *This Underpopulated World of Ours.*"

He elaborated, "What many, if not most, nations need to make full use of resources and achieve a higher living standard is not fewer workers, but more."

Finally, he and his co-workers have been vindicated after hard work against ignorance and arrogance, applying the science of yesterday to our society of today.

May it be true, as some think, that to every need tirelessly presented and solidly backed, there is a response, a fulfillment? Do modern humpty-dumpties not dare to climb walls? Is that why they never see what is on the other side?

Freedom's Gate

People trapped in civilization's spider-web have no place to land which is free, as do the birds. There is a story of two birds who loved each other so much that they forgot everything else, even themselves; even that they existed. They soared over the mountains, dived into the virile foliage of the forests and jungles, rose into the blue yonder, sang their joy to all creation.

One day the male bird found himself alone. He waited patiently awhile. Later he flew into every thicket looking. Then, he visited the houses of people, first the poor peasant houses, thinking his kindhearted mate might have gone to sing for these people so that, for a moment, they could forget their hunger. The bird was not in any of these houses.

At last, with a heavy heart, the bird sought its mate in the palatial home of a mighty prince who was known to use all things and beings for his own pleasure only, with no regard for the feelings of his subjects.

The bird-mate was there. It had been trapped and was sitting in a beautiful golden cage pining away, slowly dying, longing for its mate and not even noticing the gold bars of the cage, the expensive furniture and sumptuous room.

The distraught male bird flew back and forth outside the window through which he could see his sweetheart, but not be with her. How could he possibly help her escape?

One day, as the captive bird, as usual, watched her mate flying back and forth before her window, she suddenly saw him drop out of sight. She was heartbroken. Her lover was dead! She had nothing to live for any longer.

But he came back. Again he flew back and forth before her window -and then again he dropped right down, out of sight. Now the captive bird began to wonder.

When her sweetheart returned again, flew back and forth and then again dropped out of sight, she realized he must have tried to convey a message. But what?

Then she knew! Like her beloved bird-mate outside, she now dropped down and lay still on the bottom of the cage, as dead.

The prince and his family came in and saw the bird lying still on the floor of the cage.

"Oh, Shamandra, my Prince", wailed the wife, "we have killed her. The poor bird has died from sorrow and loneliness."

She took the cage to the open window, opened the little door and stuck her hand in to take out the bird she thought was dead.

The bird flew away, free, and joined its mate.

"You gave me the message," she said, "that I must die to become free."

Some interpret this story in the same vein as Solon, the Greek sage who said to Croesus, the King,

"Only behind the grave do you find happiness."

But there is a more subtle interpretation, widely held:

You must die before death to find freedom and happiness. You must play dead.

How do you play dead? And what do you gain by it? If you love, you play dead. You become so absorbed in the beloved you do not exist any more. There is no self, no feeling of a separate being. Also, if you are absorbed in a task, you play dead. If you rush into battle to defend your country, your principles, you are playing with death and you may really die, too. If you contemplate greatness, you are dead to yourself. You are lifted outside yourself.

Are you a bird in a golden cage? When you forget yourself, you become free. You may become happy. Why? Because you have become a living part of the great pulsating creation.

This is the stirring symbol of the Cross: Where your little self is nailed to the cross and dies, your larger, wider self comes to life.

Those friends from a previous chapter on war, who had come

to accept what happened to them with such equanimity that even bestial torture no longer affected them, had "died before death", and very effectively so. However, even in your daily work, on the assembly line in the office, you may profitably practice this art. When you no longer worry about what the man next to you makes an hour or a month, when his promotion history cannot excite you; when you just do your work serenely, cooperate cheerfully, you have played your petty self down; you have died before death. You are happier and more efficient; you are on your way to spiritual insight.

I hear you object. Keeping abreast of payroll and promotion histories of your associates keeps you on your toes and competitive.

Yes, that is the current superstition. However, competition in the payroll field breeds hypocrisy, yes-men and fakers. Every keen observer knows the joke of hierarchies.

Competition is profitable only in planning and building a better gadget, a more serviceable system. If society and the hierarchy rewards you - fine. But we all know that is not always the case, not even very often. There is the usual dragging of feet. Besides, who is there to judge a superior effort? Such a judge would have to be a bit superior himself. Superior to what? Whom? Superior to the general trend. And who would expect such to be on top of the hierarchy in a position to judge? That is not the way hierarchies are made. Hierarchies are made by accident or majority. And why or how would a majority put an unusual genius on top?

This talk boils down to this: No sane man will expect recognition or reward. His joy is in knowing that he has done well. Some were crucified for doing well, for being true. Be glad if you haven't been!

In the coinage and currency of your self-respect and your own inner joy, it pays to play dead even in your daily lives, in your shop, in your office. It pays to die before death. Your shop and your office are no less sacred than your church.

The very expression, "Play dead; die before death", at first suggest something slightly unpleasant, a bit ghoulish, perhaps, and so it may actually appear when you start out on this quest. As you work yourself into it, your viewpoint gradually changes until it becomes entirely different.

You are, at first, like a man living in a deep, dank cave and somebody comes along and wishes to take you out to see what he calls
sunshine, but his enthusiastic description of life under an open sky
awakens your deep suspicion of his sincerity and good faith - even
of his mental health. You think he is, in short, a nut!

But if he approaches the matter differently and talks to you about
dying, you look up: Yes, that makes sense. There are two facts of life
-death and taxes. So you go along with him. You understand and you
comply, even though the prospect seems at the time dim, at best.

Being of the type, perhaps, who will "try anything once" you go
along, mockingly, muttering to yourself.

You become deeply shaken for:

There is really a blue sky and, of all things - a sun!

That sun is so warm, so big, so radiant, you forget yourself in
your fascination.

One of the functions of forgetting is moving the debris of
unprofitable thoughts out of your mind so it may function more
smoothly. Your concept of being a lone self is debris, or becomes
debris when you focus on the wonder of creation and, for example,
one of its products, the Sun, which seems a very formidable achievement, sign-and-symbol. There is hardly room in your mind and heart
for two - the miracle of creation and yourself. So you yourself with-
draw, resign, disappear or die - so that the beauty of creation may
live or - you may prefer to say - so that your truer and deeper self
may live and act and move for the improvement of your community.

CLASHING MINDS

We, who dreamed with JFK about a greater reach of our economy - clashed with minds, and not mainly on questions of economics. Much of the resistance was connected with philosophy, with religion, with prayer and, particularly, with fear. Among opposition groups, two were distinctly discernible: Anti-Catholic Protestants who saw Kennedy as a representative of the Pope in Rome; anti-religious people, Atheists, who thought Kennedy had a religious bias, thought that he was in love with myths. Both these groups questioned Kennedy's soundness in economic thinking for the above reasons alone, without delving into the economic realities.

Not only were they wrong about Kennedy, who was far from being an ambassador from the Pope and who did not favor myths; who, in fact, respected equally all religions including the religion of Atheism but, apart from that, not one of the others who worked with him on this specific matter was a Catholic and most of us were not religious in any sense of the word.

Concepts of this nature quite frequently enter and confuse our dialogue and our efforts, so this is as good an opportunity as any to clear up current misconceptions. Religious people who "pray" do not necessarily believe in a "supernatural" being and do not usually ask favors. They are and were concerned with training and tuning their minds, just as athletes tune and train their muscles.

When I worked at North American Aviation Company, the computers were not up to standards at three in the morning, the only time they were available to the Thermal Division. We blamed our programming and made a point of writing down everything well in advance, during daytime peak conditions. When we fed this peerless pastry into our little monsters they still got sick - until one good night when everything seemed to work. Floyd, the operator, looked furtively around, then whispered into my ear,

"I prayed. Not to any of those high officials up there, you understand. I just slipped into John's erratic mind here," (he patted the computer's output snout) and established communication and, by golly, from that moment I knew things would improve for the old fox winked at me!"

Now Floyd scrutinized me sternly,

"Tomorrow night you join me! Two are better than one and you look as daft as myself."

For two whole weeks Floyd and I prayed with old John before our sessions. The results were so outstanding that we confessed, and then all joined. None of the computers ever stood us up after that. Obviously, we had stumbled on to a secret that was not known to HAL 9000 and its operator of the 2001 Space Odyssey.

Does anybody believe we engineers of the North American Aviation Company indulged in myths? We knew our own minds were tuned by these exercises and we had fun spinning myths around it all.

That is how people pray in our time. What is more: That is how many people prayed in times past, as excavations in Palestine and Egypt and India show, and preceding chapters have explained.

Do not some add the myth of a supernatural being? What if they do! What if they find this adds grace and fun and efficiency to the procedure?

However, there is a feeling among people about religion and prayer that has been soberly expressed by Bill. Bill was a tailgunner in a B-24 over Germany in 1945 and we lost that tail, with Bill in it. Bill freed himself from the fractured structure but fell ten thousand feet before his parachute would open. He landed on an American tank that took an enthused Bill right into battle,

"Boy, this is the life! Nothing ever happens up there!"

But Fred, the pilot of the plane, asked him,

"What did you do all that time waiting for the chute to open? Pray?"

"What do you take me for? A sneak?" snorted Bill. To him

prayers meant just begging favors; in his case begging for the chute to open or, if that couldn't be granted, then asking for admission to Heaven instead of that other place, and asking for either, at such short notice, seemed sneaky to Bill's fair mind.

However, small and great historical prayers were not begging favors. *The Lord's Prayer* was coined long ago, yet is subtler than what you may have at high-priced psychiatrists' couches.

The opening phrase,

"Our Father who art in Heaven" pinpoints the addressee. Until Freud came along, almost everybody used to like his father. OUR Father, the Father of all of us, should be a focusing point whether a mythical figure to those who so prefer - or, to others, just an image. "Who art in Heaven" provides the address. We may not know all about Heaven but we feel it should be a pleasant place or we make it a pleasant place. Our mouths water, our hearts flip-flop; we view the world like a day in May when we are in love. So far we haven't begged for a thing.

"Hallowed be Thy Name. . ." More tuning, more beauty; myths if you like, or not if you don't, and still no begging.

"Thy Kingdom come. . ." Kingdoms are ripe with beauty, glamour and the good things of life, though no begging.

"Thy Will be done. . ." Here, by degrees, you have been coaxed into accepting a collective will other than your limited own, and this is a crucifixion upon which follows a resurrection. Still no begging.

"On Earth as it is in Heaven . . ." So we have expanded our area and are down on Earth, which we know better than that place up there, and of which we are a part.

"Give us this day our daily bread." Here comes the first bit of begging and it isn't exuberant, no million dollars - just the food we need and just for today. Good chance this request will be granted and give us confidence for the next.

"And forgive us our debts. . ." This is a pleasant prospect but it has caused some to not pay the money they owe. In the old days it was called trespasses or sometimes it was called sin or mistakes or yielding to temptations and if we can still take it in this sense, we may have more success than if we stopped paying our money debts.

"As we forgive our debtors. . ." This, too, becomes easier if we take it in the old sense of forgiving insults, injustices, jabs and gossip. Taken in this sense, we would free ourselves of worry, anger and resentment.

"And lead us not into temptation. . ." Here we form our wish or determination into a request to that mythical Father or imagined Friend, or creator of us, and thus we make our resolve quite strong and definite. We have overcome, certainly in part.

"But deliver us from evil . . ." My Lutheran Bishop uncle added: "And save me from those who *bother me*." Thus concretizing a happy thought.

"For Thine is the Kingdom and the Power and the Glory forever. ..."By renouncing these attractive things yourself but hanging them onto your Beloved Father, you still have some access to them. At least, you are heir to them and feel comforted.

Some feel so attached to this prayer that trying anything else seems to them treason. Others wish to adjust their lives, thoughts, prayers if you will, to this present age, its concepts, its physics, its computers. When this century was in its teens, a group of people in San Francisco composed a set of prayers they thought would satisfy their wishes and their needs. The group included many races, colors of skin, areas and degrees of education and, of course, both sexes. One was a clergyman. some were initiates of the ancient order of sufis. Bob Considine, Hearst columnist, learned about the prayers and proposed that one of them should be used in the United Nations since it encompassed all known religions. The Russians objected: They did not want any prayer at all.

One of the group's offerings was a short morning prayer, to be voiced concurrently with breathing. A bit of fresh air early in the morning was felt to be a good beginning of any day. Then:

"BELOVED. . ." You stop, think, feel after that first word. Who is beloved? By whom? Without waiting for any answer yet, you let this one first word float enticingly in space and inside you, embracing you, bit by bit assuring you that every atom component of your body, of your surroundings, is beloved and loving; also the tiny thought components of your mind, feeling components of your heart. So your morning is new, your whole day is new and fresh, lovely and beloved! Cascades of fluid love course through your veins, circulate through your nerves, make you new and whole and incomparable and interlocked and interjoyed with all; with your friends and so-called enemies; with the whole.

And who is so compassionately loving all these atom components and thought and feeling components and friends, enemies and stars?

That lover must be whoever or whatever created all these things and beings, for why, otherwise, would It have taken on this gigantic task?

Who is this creating giant? Looking deeply into myself, could I possibly be involved? Being both creature and creator? And what shall we call It? The second word of that morning prayer suggests,

"LORD. . ."

It is a much-used word for this sort of thing and, perhaps, it is a good idea to use familiar words - and let any new aspect we want to introduce be expressed by associations and environment. For example, the word LORD alone may be a bit scary like a servant would feel toward a rude and abrupt lord and master. But after our loving introduction in which we identify with this new Lord, he has taken on the close and dear look of one who is already part of us, closer than a brother, sister or lover.

Come the third and fourth words,

"Almighty God. . ." If those two words had come first, there would have been a distance; cool, possibly insurmountable! We made the acquaintanceship the right way through a lovely loving and beloved Lord whom, we now find, is the very same as the Almighty God, whom we did not know before because we had kept Him on a pedestal, high and dry and remote! Now we begin to suspect we ourselves are part of Him and He of us.

"Through the rays of the Sun. . ."

That mighty sun! Hot, beyond imagination, but its heat diffused so we can enjoy it and benefit from it - what a magnificent sign and symbol of the mighty Creator! So, also, thought many of the old-timers, who by scholars are now classified as "sun-worshipers"

- a term encompassing a greater variety of wisdom, knowledge and maturity than our encyclopedia convey. In this morning prayer our magnificent sun becomes creature, creator - and self.

"Through the waves of the air. . ."

The air is what we find around the earth. It belongs to Earth, clothes earth in an evanescent veil which defuses the sun rays, protects us and Earth from their stings and lets through what we need. The whole Earth is a sun dependency and the Earth is us and we are the Earth - more so than is often understood. More mighty suns and more dependent planets with vast spaces between them form the universe. The following words of the prayer are,

"Through the all-pervading LIFE in space. . ."

Yes, LIFE pervades all space and that life is creature and Creator. It created us and so we ask "through the rays of the sun, through the waves of the air, through the all-pervading LIFE in space, purify and revivify us and heal our bodies, hearts and souls. . ."

Even though we are in and of that LIFE, one with it; yet, at this point in the prayer we dualize ourselves and think of that LIFE IN SPACE as coming to us (even though we are it) and purify, revivify and heal us. It sometimes is a little easier to think of it that way. In fact, it is so much easier that most religions and their sects today think only in dual terms and have forgotten the next essential step for each one as he is ready - the step to THE ONE of which each of us is a part and, potentially, the whole.

Through this morning prayer that vital step has been brought back into use. From the first whispered "beloved", one surrenders oneself to the creative forces and, in response, a flow of new, fresh life pours into you and "heals our bodies, hearts and souls." You know and feel that you are a new and whole man or woman.

The prayer that Bob Considine wanted the United Nations to adopt begins, traditionally, conventionally, with a greeting to the Master and Saviour concept in all religions,

"Most gracious Lord, Master, Messiah, and Saviour of Humanity. . ." There you've got the address.

"We greet Thee with all humility. . ." Here, you've moved yourself into the picture, in a dualistic sense so far.

"Thou art the first cause and the last effect, the Divine Light and the Spirit of Guidance, Alpha and Omega. . ." The beginning, the ending, the contents and the time span are properly pin-pointed.

"Thy Light is in all forms, Thy Love in all beings. . ." Here are the how and the where: In all forms, including yours; in all beings among whom are you. Thus, slyly, we merge, changing from two, to ONE.

". . . in a loving mother . . ." Yes, the mother is the first to merge, to slip into that sacred one-ness. Then comes the father,

"In a kind father. . ." Then follow others,

"In an innocent child, in a helpful friend, in an inspiring teacher!" So all these are part of that Spirit of Guidance, that Alpha and Omega, that most gracious Lord, Master and Saviour of Humanity?

"Allow us to recognize Thee in all Thy holy names and forms, as Rama, as Krishna, as Shiva, as Buddha. Let us know Thee as Abraham, as Solomon, as Zarathustra, as Moses, as Jesus, as Mohammed and in many other names and forms known and unknown to the world. . ."

Thus, have we gradually been allowed to recognize, through this prayer, the Spirit in all things and beings, including the holy beings and this is why compassionate Bob Considine wanted this prayer to inspire and enlighten the United Nations.

There remains for us to see the moving of the Spirit, the religions through time, past, present and future, so the prayer goes on:

"We adore Thy past. Thy Presence deeply enlightens our being and we look for Thy blessing in the future. . ."

Past and future - yes; everybody has heard about the great ones of the past and the great ones expected in the future. But Presence? That Gracious Lord, that Master, Messiah and Saviour of Humanity - is He present among us here and now? Are there holy names of today too? Maybe we better look around. And within.

"Oh Messenger, Christ, Prophet, sacred Chain of Enlightened Ones, Thou whose heart constantly reaches upward, Thou comest on Earth with a Message when Humanity decayeth and speakest the Word that is put into Thy mouth as the light filleth the crescent moon. . ."

Is this how it happens? When the relationship between us humans decayeth, when wisdom recedes, then a messenger is chosen to bring the good word that is put into his mouth? To revivify and reaffirm that ancient truth and bugle?

"Let the Star of the Divine Light shining in Thy Heart be reflected in the hearts of Thy devotees . . . "

Is that how the Message is kindled in hearts and then spreads and causes the smitten to chant these last words of the prayer?

"May the Message of God reach far and wide and make the whole Humanity One single brotherhood in the Fatherhood of GOD."

According to the annals of the prophets of millenniums the preceding prayer is directed, not to the One and Only Creator, but to a specific aspect of Him: The prophets' prophet, the Teachers' teacher, the aspect that eagerly preaches, persuades and implores man to follow the path of Wisdom, of Love, Harmony and Beauty. For the sake of practical bookkeeping. the prophets divide the religious devotees in three groups: the first, the apprentice group, begins by listening to and adoring an individual teacher. He is then a Bramachari with the Hindus and yogis, a Fana-Fi-Sheik among the Sufis, Christians, Moslems and Hebrews. By and by, the devotee advances into the next higher group as he learns to listen to and adore the entire chain of teachers, prophets and saints. He worships Christ, the Universal Spirit of whom Jesus is an example, or the Boddhisattva among the Buddhists (The Lord Matreya, the female version of Quan Yin). Among the Sufis he is a Fana-fi-Rassoul. Finally, he soars so far and high he can only worship God himself, the Creator, the Unfathomable. He is an "Enlightened One" among the Buddhists; a "Yogachari" among the yogis, a "Fana-fi-Allah" among the Sufis.

In real life, man's evolution does not often pass through such prim stages. Many an infant worships God, the undefined and compassionate Spirit and some go through their entire lives worshipping only God the Creator and never the God-man, the Messenger, nor the individual teacher. Among scientists, particularly, we frequently find this type. To suggest that these need to come down on their knees to worship any certain name or form is like insisting that in the gardens of Earth there should be only orange trees, no other kind.

In a sense, all prayers as so far explained touch merely the surface. There is a world yet to explore, connected with what a limping branch of science terms subconscious, or unconscious, or superconscious. By repeating certain well-chosen words or phrases again and again, whimsical weaklings have turned into radiant power sources. If breathing is included and postures or rhythmic movement, the effect may be multiplied. Such procedures transform prayers into sacred practices, meditation, contemplation. These are essential tools of education which must immediately be added to the usual dosage of reading, writing and the shocking number of "essential subjects" now being taught in schools and universities, monopolizing the claim to "Education". In the following, therefore, we summarize what may be termed silent reach.

SILENT REACH

The consensus of studied opinion is always wrong. This statement was made by Charles F. Kettering on the occasion of his receiving an award of merit from the American Alumni Council in July 1948. Charles Kettering was one of our most remarkable inventors, the kind, it is said, who made America. So the Council of Alumni from our universities conveyed upon him this honor and he used the occasion to speak, as follows, on the education which these well-intentioned donors had pursued:

"The kid, from the time he enters kindergarten or maybe a little farther up is examined two or three times a year and, of course, if he flunks, that's awful. An inventor flunks all the time and if he succeeds once, he's in."

Mr. Kettering concludes that our education builds on fear - the fear of failure, and chokes creative faculties. Today the most striking proof of this contention is the thunderous barrage from all news media about our "inflation" and the commiserations about "the mess of the nation's economy," that we have "overstepped our potentials" and have to "slow down or become ruined."

Actually, the U.S. economy has never been better. In addition, we could, at this time, have a considerably higher standard of living and general economic activity, and without any inflation, if we so choose. The experts and non-experts who realize this are the few who ignored the fear that Education tried to instill, those who conform to the "inventor mind" which Charles Kettering wrote about. They have that inborn "Silent Reach" which was once deemed as an exclusive achievement by religion. If it ever was, it isn't now, except that a few clerics have it along with some inventors. Currently, it is claimed by psychiatry which does not have it yet in any broad sense, though a few individual psychiatrists do.

A San Franciscan learned about it through his stomach, the reason being that while his midsection was sore, his mind was clear. So his doctor told him that with such a mind he should be able to do his own thing, dispense with dreary drugs and pills. The doctor couldn't offer him professional aid of the kind he was contemplating but asked if he didn't know somebody who had fooled around with Yoga. The San Franciscan looked up a friend who knew him well and also had traveled in the deep spaces where Yoga and similar arts are found. The San Franciscan was taught the attitudes, practices and subtleties that in a few weeks overcame the rebellion of his stomach.

What is this silent reach? Charles Kettering probably did not even know the word yoga. This is just one among many names. Every known civilization had a try at it, though the art has never been fully mastered. Many practitioners feel the art has been slowly declining during the past millenniums, and that it is now gradually picking up again, but hasn't yet reached the level of a few thousand years ago. Some speculate that the future apex of yoga will be in California!

Any book about improvements, in relationships, in economics would be woefully incomplete without touching this age-old human talent of Silent Reach. This may be summarized without detailing any one school or approach. The basic principles are simple, practical and may guide the practitioner further than the often cumbersome methods of traditional schools.

The child who roams forests, beaches and mountains and learns of the way of wild animals, birds, plants and trees has his first lesson in the art of life and of his own mind. He may roam alone, or with good friends who help him in his quest, or again with playmates who hamper his progress by throwing at him uncouth ingredients of our now-side-tracked society.

Then, at six, when he may be at the threshold of achievement, when he begins to glimpse the magnificence of the subtler world, he is yanked out of his woods and meadows and put through a school that teaches him the tricks of civilization, but along with that task, also, often crushes what is most promising in him and wastes his time with memory games and the unpromising history of human follies.

The most important cause now for the preservation of the race is to bend the schools in the direction that some foundation-sponsored experimental schools and some Montessori schools have already begun. In these schools the child is listened to, his special talents are drawn out and he is encouraged to follow and develop these talents almost exclusively. The school is built around the pupil and not devoted to filling young minds with trivia.

As that San Franciscan with his once-sore stomach showed us, even people who have passed through the ordeal of our schools may still develop awareness and "Union" or "Yoga". It may be best to begin at the age of eight as the Yogis recommend, or even before birth as the Sufis prefer, but if you haven't started that early, just begin any time!

Like a selected astronaut, you step out from your narrow mind, your feelings and your body - out into the wide open space. From out there you look in at what you may call your personality. This stepping outside may be a revelation in itself. You see, at once, that you are none of these things; they are your possessions and you can make of them what you want. They are your servants. If at any moment any of these servants try to give the idea he is not a servant, you better make him realize that he is!

As you step outside, some shortcomings immediately show up. Certain thoughts or worries come drifting into your mind and you greet them - you, their master - though not a brutal master. You ask what they want and if their explanation is not too clear, you dismiss them. You may also watch your body, its posture, its muscles or fat and decide on a few corrections and then undertake to make those corrections, though this may take weeks or months. Sooner or later, you may be aware of your breathing. In the forests or meadows you may have acquired the habit of breathing noiselessly, smoothly, in order not to scare little animals. Noiseless breathing is usually good breathing. You may also be aware of the rhythm breathing gives to your system. Breathing is not just shoving out polluted air and pulling in the fresh variety. Breathing is the rhythm that connects you with the vast breathing universe, the Creator and His Creation.

Breathing synchronously with another person may at a certain stage in your development and in his, help both of you to think synchronously, facilitating thought-communication without words or physical signs. Similarly, breathing may strengthen and clarify your link to the all-soul which some of us call God and which others would say is just an aspect of God.

These things are taught and practiced at certain stages by Yogis, Sufis and other groups.

Yogis specialize. A Hatha Yogi teaches postures of the body and the influence of these postures on gland secretion and other bodily functions. He may give a schizophrenic a straining bend that will release juices that may gradually heal. He gives his pupils exercises in postures and breathing that eventually may develop trends and powers for which western science has, so far, no explanation. Through this one system, Hatha Yoga, a student may rise all the way to states usually connected with other branches of yoga, for the different approaches lead to the same general achievements. Hatha Yoga progressively affects the mind, while Gnana Yoga is the name of a system dealing more directly with the mind, a "scientist's yoga". For a person of devotion or deep feeling "Bhakti yoga" is a more likely system; while for a man or woman of action, a soldier, business woman or statesman, "Karma yoga" is the thing, the "yoga of action". The karma yogi develops and achieves through his action. The "mantram" yogi achieves through repetition of sacred phrases, "mantrams". "Raya Yoga", "Kriya Yoga" are based on meditation and breath control and are, in a sense, a blending of the other systems. There are other yoga practices taught by Buddha and by the Chinese and Japanese sages.

The sufis are mostly grouped, not according to purpose or system; simply by origin, like the previously mentioned Mevlevis. There are others, such as the Nakshibandis, the Tasawufs and the Chishti Order, established by the mystic Moinuddin Chishti. This was brought to America and later to Europe by the Hindu musician and mystic Inayat Khan, who gradually developed a unique "Sufi Message", embracing all religious and mystical endeavor and firmly planted in our modern world.

The sufi aspirant does not need to make up his mind in advance whether he should walk the Hatha, Gnana, Bhakti or Karma path, as most yogi aspirants do. A sufi teacher chooses for him, guides him, until he knows. Sometimes this procedure is also employed among yogis.

Through any proper sufi or yoga training one becomes more keenly aware of one's own mind, feelings, body functions. One senses and develops man's innate power, one senses the limitations, the interconnections between all these parts of oneself. One begins to know one's own being, becomes happier, more well-balanced and efficient. One may or may not increase one's income and rank. A rise or fall in the social and business world is illusive, a phantom, never under organized control from anywhere. The trained persons take all that with a knowing smile. Worldly success, while appreciated, does not mean so much to them any more. It is the inner stature that matters. It is understanding that matters, understanding of others, of one's self.

Occasionally a Sufi or Yoga student may develop communication of thought and feeling from himself to others or from others to himself without recourse to words It is doubtful whether this is due to training or to natural talents. There may even be communication with what is called "spirits". This is always discouraged by genuine yoga or sufi teachers because of unreliability of the spirit world and because of the danger. The danger is that spirits may so dominate a communicator that he loses control of his own mind and heart, temporary at first, though permanent damage may well develop.

Even the simple practice of emptying your mind of all thought may lead to spirit entry and later domination. The emptying of the mind is a practice often prescribed by a teacher who, if he considers himself "competent", then believes he can gauge any pupil's capability and properly determine the duration of his meditation or practices.

Who is a competent teacher? Why is he competent?

Before a lawyer or an engineer or doctor is permitted to practice he has to be given a license by an authority who tests his ability. This test does not really guarantee performance. With yogi and sufi teachers similar credentials exist, provided by some school or group. The basis of these credentials are less known. Even the best-informed can only guess. Therefore, the only criterion here is the faith of the individual who subjects himself to being taught.

Most modern pupils of this sort of teacher end up vacillating between sky-high faith and the darkest doubts, dutifully hiding their vacillations under a mantle of firm assurances. The doubts fester into suspicion; balance and tranquility are lost; the very basis for sound advancement is shattered.

The answer in most cases is: Teach yourself, at least in the beginning. The need for teachers is greatly exaggerated in any and all fields today. Many have gone all the way and fully realized their potentials without the aid of any direct teacher. In the beginning, at least, train on your own. If you haven't the strength to teach yourself, it is a fair bet you won't do well with a teacher either. Often the teacher becomes a substitute for effort; in other words, he becomes a substitute for achievement.

Have you already set aside a few moments - no more than five minutes at first - at the beginning of your day, or at the end, or preferably both? Are you really ambitious, wanting to set that first period at about three in the morning, such an atrocious time of night that you feel you deserve a whopping inspiration? At that time, say the pundits, magnetic currents are auspicious.

Do you sit in bed or on a chair, back straight, head well back; breathing rhythmically and with as little noise as comfortably possible? Do you like to begin with a prayer to tune in, one of those in a previous chapter, for example? Are you looking at your thoughts and feelings now, greeting them, playing with them, pondering their origin? Then throwing them out? As they come sneaking back, do you greet them again without rancor and ask your mind if this is the best it can do, or if it would try to control and sort that flow?

Do you feel improvement? Then, do you concentrate for a few moments on objects or ideas that appeal to you? Do you allow your mind to run around their surfaces or main concepts? Do you exclude, for the time being, objects or ideas that are repellant or indifferent to you? Later, you may consider such subjects; not in the beginning.

Is the alluring prospect of mastery shimmering before you? Then, do you pass in review before you persons you wish to get along with; business connections, family, social friends? Do you present vivid pictures of these persons in your mind and think through likely meetings and talks with them? Through these contacts with people in your visions, in your day-dreaming, do you prepare and improve knowledge of them, your attitude to them, your attitude in general?

If you have acquired a new, more enjoyable attitude to people, do you begin to feel and reach the Creator of the people? Do you sense that the path to this Creator goes through His Creation, Man?

A venerable saint put it this way, "My action toward any man I think of as my action toward the Maker of men and any man's action toward me I consider that Maker's action."

The same Saint said, "He who worships the Creator and despises His creation worships in vain."

Striving alone along this path of achievement, many a time you may pray and hope for a personal teacher. But if you do not find one you may have a greater satisfaction: You may find an intuition developing in you that makes you more efficiently your own teacher. Don't spoil it by naming this intuition a "spirit", which really would be an intruder. You may call it God or your inner self. But if you call it a "spirit" you may end up getting just that and become completely side-tracked.

On the other hand, you may avail yourself of many little tricks to hasten your advance and develop your intuition - head-rolling for example. Coming out from a head-rolling session in a little garden bungalow in Suresnes, a working man's suburb of Paris, I noted to my companion - a hardworking chemical engineer -"If someone had looked in the window he would have thought we were crazy."

His reply, "We are."

Why, oh why, do busy men spend minutes of their precious

working day rolling their heads around on the necks like some machine part out of kilter?

Well, neck muscles are among the least used in our daily routine so exercising them is meritorious. A part from that, some "competents" tell us the circling of the head creates a strong magnetic space current sucking superfluous ideas from us out into space and permitting essential, undogmatic life-and-energy currents to enter our little systems. Reassuring, isn't it?

While embarrassed Westerners perform these exercises within closed bungalows or bedrooms, curtains drawn, insouciant Easterners - sufis, yogis and many others - sit shamelessly out on the sidewalks and let their heads circle boldly. Some Africans even circle their entire torsos.

With the movements there are thoughts,

This unworthy gadget under my head (and including it) is not 'my' body. It is (or will promptly become) the Temple of God! (Nod, nod, nod, affirmative).

and: "These thoughts criss-crossing my humble gray matter are not my thoughts. They are the thoughts of God. (Or will soon be.)"

and, "This heart I feel within my chest, a seat of feelings, is not my heart. It is the shrine of God."

What can you expect after a lifetime of such affirmations, confirmed by a whirling and nodding head?

As it is said, so be it.

If you are an active person and don't like to sit while you think and affirm, you may do it walking. You may walk between skyscrapers or among trees, dedicating your body, mind and heart - and the skyscrapers or the trees - to that creator of skyscrapers or at least of trees, and of us. You breathe rhythmically, creatively while so walking. That's what those ancient warriors did in Jericho. Blowing on horns was just a feint. The power that made the walls fall was this silent, sacred dedication.

What has been achieved through the thousands of years yogis and sufis developed and studied the results of their movements, head-rollings, postures, breathings and mantrams? We don't know at all. Any one may call himself a yogi, sufi or avatar. That does not mean that he has any information on the real achievements in these fields. But MDs of many nations are now eagerly checking, and not only pompous doctors looking down their noses but vigorous, vital men and women who accepted discipleship in order to receive pertinent information. Some even ventured neck-breaking excursions into wild mountain regions where knowledgeable hermits dwell.

What is the purpose of this many-splendoured effort? To reach further into the dark recesses of our thoughts and emotions - that super-computer-plus - where dwell the solutions to all our social, economic, international and personal problems and ambitions.

THIS UNFINISHED BUSINESS

The move to survey the nation's potentials, initiated during the Kennedy Administration, remained unfinished at the termination of that administration. It is still unfinished today. The participants are not solely to blame; the nation's economy as a whole is also unfinished business. The succession of governments are not to blame any more than the population as a whole, of which the governments are but a small fraction, and no less efficient than the rest. It is simply that, except for a few prophets crying in the wilderness, nobody has taken the trouble to look at the nation as a whole in the same way as a Board Chairman looks at his company.

There are shouts about labor or business, avarice or greed, Russia or Japan causing all our trouble, though proper corrective measures could eliminate any bad effects from avarice, greed, labor, business, Japan or Russia.

Among wilderness-crying prophets who know what corrective measures could or should be taken are Dr. John H.G. Pierson, who has been at it since 1941, Dr. John Philip Wernette; who wrote his first trenchant books about these matters in the mid-forties; Dr. Leon Keyserling, Chairman of the President's Economic Council under Truman; Dr. Melville Ulmer of Maryland U; and Dr. Seymour Harris, senior advisor to the Treasury under Kennedy and Johnson.

Those of us who, under J.F. Kennedy, worked with these matters have been accused of fiddling while our cities burned; and, truly, considering our lack of success, or at least lack of completion, I accept the challenge and urgently call upon capable readers to pick up and complete what we so timidly began. As an incitement, I shall report on our loosely knit group, our tentative plans, our tiny steps.

The eager reader cannot help shouting "How much better I could have done!"

John F. Kennedy himself, I think, did not fiddle while our cities burned. He had that urge to stop, look, listen and learn, always, and, particularly, during that last unofficial mission unfolding around him. Not a trace of this effort is found in the flood of books about him, perhaps because it was not completed; possibly, also, because at first sight it appeared not very significant. It wasn't, in his usual style, about the dignity of man or freedom of choice, but simply providing the material development required for those loftier goals. Strictly speaking, it wasn't even that much, but rather showing us and himself what material potentials we had.

The loosely knit group working with him on these matters was confident that a level of production and enjoyment could be found from which profitable employment would be available for any and all willing to work. Today, this has become more creditable than it was in the Kennedy days. Private firms employing so-called "unemployables" found that these maligned individuals worked even better than the average new employee when given the chance. Our concepts and ideas have been wrong, not the people or the conditions.

Ghettoes, riots, vanishing gold, imbalance of payments, inflation - are all these mutually incompatible monsters, or may they all be cured sweetly, and simultaneously?

If so, what man, or what group of men, could perform such a miracle?

Nobody would have to. The basic miracle has been performed already by the industry and inventiveness of teeming millions taming a continent. The riches were here though we hadn't noticed.

What this special group around Kennedy planned to do was to set in motion a super-survey that would show us what we really owned.

Don't we know?

There are estimates varying between two and fifteen trillion dollars. All these estimates are only a rough approach to existing land and hardware. What we own, far beyond all that, are the potentials based on the latest scientific discoveries and developments. The great amount of existing surveys, partly overlapping, tell us very little about these real potential riches. Even if the existing surveys were combined, we would not have a reliable measure.

A tentative survey of the Nation's resources was tried under President Herbert Hoover and continued, with additions and adjustments under later administrations. When John F. Kennedy entered the stage, significant new developments - in science, in general, and in computerdom - had made such surveys more meaningful, more reliable and pitted for much higher stakes.

Believe it or not, even at this point objections are heard: "It isn't more material goods we need today but better morals, more spiritual values."

This may be true for limited sections of our society, as hinted in previous chapters, but the total body of a nation does not operate well if not everybody is busy working for the nation and himself. The issue is not more material goods but a balanced economy employing all who are able and willing to work. The term "able" to work does not mean conforming to present requirements of employment offices. The giant Lockheed Aerospace Company hired groups of people on the East Coast and on the West Coast who in no sense conformed to the company's employment standards. These people had been on welfare for generations. To the company's surprise they worked better and more steadfastly than the average new employee conforming with the rules of employment on every point.

Also, there is a superstition around that our "highly sophisticated working place requires skills beyond what some unemployed can offer."

On the contrary, the technical revolution has created many more jobs that require no skill at all. The people hired by Lockheed had neither skills nor much education. There is always room for the specialist, of course. At the same time, there is more and more room for the completely unskilled - or will be, as soon as employment offices have learned the lessons of the latest experiments.

I have been jumping a few years ahead of the Kennedy story. This was to show how right the Kennedy people were in their assumption, and to show how much better prepared we are now, today, for continuing their work.

The economists, industrialists and engineers working unofficial-
ly on these matters benefited from the advice and encouragement
of Administration officials, scholars and business men all over the
nation.

The contemplated survey, one-pointed in composition and aim,
may be looked at from five different angles for better understanding of its multipurpose. It may be called five surveys combined and
integrated into one.

The first might be called an inventory; inventory, not only of
things but of potentials - what we could have if we wanted, with
present capabilities of science and technology. All such resources
of this nation would be listed, whether used here or exchanged,
through trade, for supplies from abroad. This survey, then, would
include the new and amazing gadgets and systems science has been
dreaming about that "could be built within the technology but not
the money available today". Why touch it at all if we "don't have the
money?" First, because this is a list of things, not money. At a later
stage in the survey we may even find that the money-bogeyman was
not so monstrous as we have been accustomed to thinking.

The second survey is about people, man power. Here "man power" means just the power of a man (or woman) - any one. Would not
his training, education and life history, including his good record, be
featured? Perhaps, but with tongue-in-cheek, for recent experience
has shown that our beliefs in these matters have, to a surprising degree, been superstition. Also, the rapid change in today's technology
has entirely changed the aspect of training. Often a man's training is
obsolete before he is through with his course. Training is still useful
for sharpening of the mind, or acquiring good working habits, less
and less for learning methods. These, more and more, have to be
acquired at work week by week, day by day. This new fact favors the
direct employment of any and all without the cumbersome pretraining we thought so necessary a while ago. This pretraining was always
a headache, for how could you raise the enthusiasm and cooperation
of a man who for years had been unemployed, unwanted - by suggesting to him that if he applied himself at training school, he might

get satisfactory employment.

A look at today's working place demonstrates the changing character of "training" even up to the most responsible positions. Men without any degrees direct complicated aerospace work at some of our largest companies. They have worked themselves up to become the most versatile experts. Study courses and degrees may still have their meaning but in a changing and possibly reduced sense.

Two valid questions should be asked prospective employees today: First, what does he want to do? Lack of general knowledge on the part of the applicant may make it difficult for him to answer even that question without first learning what choices there are. Second: How decisive an effort is he willing to put into doing what he wants to do? This is one thing a conscientious employer has a right to ask and must ask: Is the employee willing to give all he has? And this is all an employee can ever promise.

The third survey concerns customer desires. This comes close to what is called "market analysis". In this present market analysis, all citizens are customers and all goods are offered. It isn't a question of finding out whether a particular product will sell, but which products, among many, should be produced and in what approximate amount. The task is a bit more complex than a usual market analysis. With present computers it is feasible. The first task of this survey is to inform - inform all citizens about what they may have: The amazing rather unknown things science has now made available or can make available. This first part will be an information and/or education period.

Among the customers who should be informed and then asked what they want, would also be public bodies such as the Defense Department, the Department of Education and Welfare, the Commerce Department and state, city and county governments.

On the basis of the three preceding surveys the jig-saw puzzle of production, including research and services, would now be put into operation as the fourth survey task. This is more complex than the previous tasks, though the technological aspects are manageable, at least according to Norbert Weiner, the venerable father of computerdom who advised us just before he passed away. What makes this fourth task particularly difficult are the disagreements and quarrels that would arise as to whether we need a new race track or a new super-carrier or new Ghetto enterprises. The people most able to decide wisely, meaning to the benefit of most people, are economists and scientists. They can usually see how each enterprise would affect employment and the total economy. But would these experts be permitted to make the decisions? Hardly. Even if they were, would they always be right? Not always, and not altogether, but they would have a better chance of being closer to the right answer.

There are already at this time general objections to the described surveys. America, it is said, is a country of individualists, each one forging his own fate, not a slave of surveys and mass production.

Beautiful thoughts and true, for a small percentage of citizens, and for almost everybody sixty years ago. Our associations of humans, generally speaking, has become quite different today. At this date almost all of us (and we did not have a choice as to whom) are dependent upon united efforts. Our work, our food and shelter, all the things we need and want come to us from work benches and factories over which we have scant, if any, control. We accept the work we are offered if we want to work at all. We see the beautiful cooperative pattern, although we have very little control of it. Nevertheless, there is beauty, there is hope and there is romance in this half-hidden, less-than-half-understood cooperative giant we are working in and with, and which we are exploring a little further in these pages in the hope that we may recognize it for what it is.

So if we are to progress, which today may well mean if we are to survive, we must complete this fourth survey, agree on main principles, map projects in production, services and research in sufficient number to offer employment for all comers including those wanting to change jobs, those seeking a wider scope for their ambition.

What would happen to present enterprises if those who don't like their jobs would quit for more alluring projects?

When a person wants to leave a job the feeling is usually mutual: The job also wants to leave him. He feels and knows he is not really needed; he is not being an essential part of his organization. The company will usually benefit from his leaving as much as he will. The company does not always know this in advance. A situation which may be called a worker's market, a market in which each worker has a wide choice, tends to benefit not just the worker but general management efficiency. Alert management has long suspected this. The final result might prove a pleasant surprise to everybody.

The fifth and final survey would be financing - of enterprises for which our surveys have determined that we have resources, man power and a reasonable need. These are the criteria for sound financing of any undertaking and it would not be difficult to find solutions - many solutions. The difficulty would be agreeing on any one solution. There are strong opinions and ugly scare words in the area of money and finance. Prejudice has played the greatest part in preventing sound advance. After carefully researching the large field of possibilities, we might possibly end up with a number of solutions and try each one of them for various groups of enterprises. Such a procedure may ensure better overall cooperation than trying to stick to one single solution.

From beginning to end, a preponderance of private companies must take the brunt of this probing research, with governments providing liaison and information. In all cases, so far, in which hard-core welfare recipients, even "unemployables" have been successfully and lastingly employed, private companies have been the employers, particularly from the aerospace industries and banking. Government agencies tried, with the best of intentions, but were hamstrung by rigid rules and red tape. This is to be expected. Any public body is exposed to so much suspicion, criticism and harassment that there is bound to be "overcontrol". For cohesion, government participation in the program is nevertheless necessary.

To many people who consider themselves well informed in a general sense, our entire presentation may give rise to serious questions: We haven't so far had to survey our entire capabilities in order to prosper and be happy. And even if we do, now, how do we know the financing can be scaled up to any desired level as long as there are resources, manpower and a reasonable need? Why is all this necessary and how do we know it will work? Has there been any change in the U.S. material development that warrants such a new approach?

Yes, there has. The change has been decisive and even momentous, but has come along so gradually that many have failed to notice it. There was a time when the United States was a geographically-expanding continent. "Go West, Young Man!" This vast, expanding continent could absorb almost any ambitious scheme, enterprise, idea; almost any number of new, eager immigrant workers.

The geographical expansion has ceased long ago. There is, at present, an even greater field of expansion provided by those miracles: Science, technology, cybernetics. The nature of this expansion is such that it can be demonstrated and exploited through sophisticated surveys using advanced computer systems, thoughtful programming, alternative mathematical approaches - and only through such approaches can this potential expansion be discovered and utilized. Luckily, in this art the USA is well ahead. Unluckily, we are reluctant to use our fine systems for this essential task. We use these fine systems for trivia and sometimes we use them for tasks that are not at all suited for such treatment; for example, for trying to determine how many people would die in a nuclear attack or which weapons' systems to choose among various alternatives, or how to conduct the war in Vietnam. In these cases, a highly exact method is used for calculating matters that cannot be determined with any degree of accuracy. We begin with crude guesswork which we feed into high-grade machines. Out comes nothing but cruder guesswork. clothed in a false halo of "accuracy".

Some of the Kennedy people took part in these ridiculous exercises. Others, at least, had the good sense for the first time to apply the computer systems to the essential tasks of economic and financial organization as here reported.

What is almost miraculous is that the principles underlying these efforts were understood and even proposed by a succession of American statesmen who lived long before computers were in use. Ben Franklin was perhaps the first. All through his long life he listened and learned, as well as taught. He listened and he gave advice at the court of Louis XVI when France was fighting for its life or its sanity just before the revolution when the vilest crooks were trying to wreck her economy. He compared this intricate game with the simpler patterns at home in the colonies and thus formulated his mature economic philosophy which is available in the Library of Congress. Abraham Lincoln's comprehensive views and sharp analyses are quoted increasingly among modern economists. More recently, banker and Senator Robert L. Owen, Federal Reserve Board Chairman Mariner Eccles and, stretching into the Kennedy era, Alan Sproul, past President of the New York Federal Reserve Bank; and last, but not least, Dr. John Philip Wernette - have prepared and launched the economic philosophy underlying the effort described here. Among the nation's economists there is now, finally, such general agreement that Dr. Seymour Harris said to me last time we met, "Ninety per cent of U.S. economists now agree."

In addition to economists, almost every trade and profession and the most common and uncommon experiences were represented on the work team. Arthur Schlesinger, the historian, was a livewire throughout this work. Many of us had actual experience with so-called "unemployables" at home and/or abroad.

The estimates and forecasts of this multi-experienced team have been handsomely firmed up by pertinent experiences in later years.

Some of the people in the Kennedy group had worked on financial developments and recovery after wars in Europe and Asia and thoroughly enjoyed playing the more flexible fields of the larger American economy, which offered so much vaster potentials than did any other nation's. These people were also concerned and surprised at the many Americans who seemed totally ignorant of the resiliency of their own nation's economy. Many Americans, if they looked out over our virgin forests some centuries ago and heard someone propose building what we now have (cities, factories, homes; our America today) would have exploded, "Are you crazy? Where'd the money come from?"

With so many others they think of money as a set sum neatly contained in a jar, while modern money is figures in books. Some fifty years ago there were about fifteen billion dollars so represented. Today there are several hundred billions. Where did the addition come from? Gifts from France or England? Didn't these people ever read Mariner Eccles or John Philip Wernette?

All this additional money was created on the books as and when our material wealth was built, through the established banking practices which enable us to match, in money, any level of expenditure as long as there is balance between output and input - exactly what our surveys would try to establish. Gauging resources, manpower, needs - cannot always be done accurately. But mistakes can always be corrected. The fact that we did try, and later corrected, is the reason we have a United States today.

There is nothing strikingly new in all this, though a culmination is just now taking place in a process that has been going on for some years. There was a time in the early history of our nation when enterprises were thrusts into a vast vacuum. Success was almost certain if the effort was sound and sustained. When maturity or completeness approached, it became increasingly difficult to judge the prospects of any new enterprise. Overall planning became, first, desirable and later mandatory in the single enterprises, then industry-wide. Finally, it became necessary to plan nationally. Many look with romantic eyes to the past and doubt the new. But Romance has proved to be with us still, today, as demonstrated in so many surveys through which Americans proved their ability to stick with their expressed intentions and thus bolster and improve the general economy. Just after World War II manufacturers launched surveys to find out what their prospective customers wanted. Then they unleashed their producing giants and found, to their satisfaction, that everybody bought almost exactly as they had indicated.

There is a conviction in certain quarters that full employment equates uncontrolled inflation. One reason for this conviction is that full-employment usually happened during inherently inflationary periods such as major wars, when accelerated production was scheduled regardless of economic considerations, and, notably, production of goods that were not consumed: Weapons and munitions. The full employment issue, including the relationship between full employment and inflation, has been researched for more than thirty years not just from an ivory tower, but by economists thoroughly grounded in national as well as international economic policy, such as Dr. John H.G. Pierson. His findings have been presented in a great number of articles and four books, now classics in this field. Building upon the congressional *Employment Act* of 1946, Dr. Pierson would have Congress guarantee full employment and the appropriate level of consumer spending every year, with correctional safeguards. This is not only feasible today but would greatly benefit business, labor, and the nation as a whole, as well as the now unemployed. A few quotes from his recent writings would highlight his plan. In the *Honolulu Advertiser* of March 27, 1970:

"From the over-all economic standpoint guaranteed full employment would make recessions impossible and inflation highly unlikely, paradoxical as that may seem. First, the employment and consumer spending guarantees would have ceilings as well as floors to restrain inflation from the side of demand and prevent the price-wage spiral. Secondly, because the government was offering such guarantees it would be in a position to persuade business, labor and farm leaders to agree to follow some reasonable set of guidelines in establishing their selling prices so that "cost push" inflation would be restrained too.

"Here lies the explanation of that seeming paradox - the reason why the outright guaranteeing of full employment, far from representing a 'well-intentioned but impractical' goal, would itself provide the best cure for inflation."

In the *Washington Post* 14 May 1972, during the Presidential primaries, "The candidates are setting their economic sights too low." He subsequently quotes the various candidates' statements about wanting to establish full employment. Finally, he includes the Democratic platform of 1968 and comments: 'Without explanation of how it can be accomplished, this does little more than widen the credibility gap.' The *Congressional Record* 1 March 1972 outlines Dr. Pierson's entire plan and will be submitted as an appendix after this chapter. Here we quote a paragraph that shows the width and breadth and depth of this proposal,

"A word is needed about what is really at stake because the arguments over the full employment issue are often pitched on altogether too-narrow ground. In briefest summary: 1) Involuntary unemployment is destructive of personality; 2) An assurance of continuous prosperity and full employment would weaken the anti-social (usually inflationary) compulsions of business, labor, farmer and other interest groups. 3) Racial peace seems impossible in this country without universal job opportunity, the present lack of which is also partly responsible for the alienation of youth, not to speak of the helpless bitterness of many older people. 4) Getting rid of poverty would be greatly simplified as a result of the cash income effects of continuous full employment (more paid labor; less chance of exploiting labor by paying substandard wages). 5) The extra wealth (GNP) which would be created under those full activity conditions - the staggering amount now wasted through avoidable non-production production - is needed to help finance programs to meet the problems of the cities, backward rural areas and the environment generally, including again problems of poverty but not limited to them. 6) Internationally, that extra wealth would confirm our ability to extend more generous aid to the world's less-developed countries. 7) More (and more fundamental) than that, confidence in our ability to maintain a market adequate for our own full employment prosperity through domestic policy would substantially deflate our fear of imports and our exaggerated preoccupation with export markets and export surpluses; thus it would enable us to be a "good neighbor" that encourages and helps the less-developed countries to shift 'from aid to trade' as they become ready for it."

Dr. Pierson does not confine himself to writing. He visits Washington, D.C. for long periods of time whenever requested or whenever he sees a chance for implementation.

Shortly after John Pierson's first book, *Full Employment*, Yale University Press, 1941, came John Wernette's crystal-clear *Financing Full Employment*, Harvard University Press, 1945, a different approach to the same general goal. In 1947 came Pierson's *Full Employment and Free Enterprise*; in 1964 *Insuring Full Employment* (Viking Press) and in 1973 *Essay on Full Employment* (Scarecrow Press).

All along, Dr. Leon Keyserling, Chairman of the President's Economic Council under Truman, has written and spoken to the same tune and is now working closely with Pierson. Dr. Melville Ulmer of Maryland University has written similarly in current magazines and newspapers, specifically in *Washington Post* 2 July 1972. Above all, Dr. Paul Samuelson, Nobel-prize-winning incomparable teacher, has plowed the same field in his classic works with the supreme independence of the proud and also humble scholar. It appears that the deeper a person delves into the Full Employment issue, the more time he spends on it, the more convinced does he become that this is a workable and profitable goal.

Completely inflation-free incidents or accidents are rare. Throughout the first half of this century the fabulous Mah family firmly imposed a placid, stagnant economy with no price fluctuations all over western China. And Sweden, in the general depression years 1930-35, kept price fluctuations within a two per cent limit happily applauded by sundry American economists - until Gunnar Myrdal came and told us the Swedes had tried their best to expand economic activity even at the expense of possible inflation, for they considered full employment and efficiently running factories more important. Since the Swedes contemplated no such devices as here described, slight inflation might have developed.

The inflation we had in the United States in the late sixties, however inconvenient, was moderate, manageable and did not constitute any forewarning of a debacle such as Germany, Brazil and other countries experienced. Now, today, a more pervasive type has developed which requires attention. Dr. Pierson's proposals, that would provide full employment along with curbing inflation, might be the best alternative to the present course. Also, the multi-surveys described above and the resulting activities would have the same double effect of curbing inflation while providing optimum employment. It would help if the reputed American passion for gadgetry could be directed towards things in surplus rather than in short supply.

In the fall of 1963, a comprehensive meeting, a giant slug-it-out-talkathon was planned, to hammer out basics, when tragedy struck.

An independent effort of the same intent and on an even broader scale, initiated by R. Buckminster Fuller, has been in operation for some years. In this "World Game", the whole globe is the playground, indicated by the term Synergy, promising a greater reach by planning both sources and requirements on a global and cross-professional scale. Another term, Ephemeralization, tells of a built-in principle of change with time, the required inconstancy of needs, preferences, institutions and thought patterns. This World Game reminds one of some specific and profound yoga traditions of the Far East of very ancient origin and holds enormous promise for man on earth.

The Kennedy-planned surveys would have formed a link to Buckminster Fuller's broad sweep. A first, sketchy survey would show in a general way what huge resources we actually have to play with and how misplaced are many of the still-prevailing rules (some call laws) inherited from a scarce economy. As a result, new enterprises in the general direction indicated by this first survey would spring up, enrich us and strengthen our resolve to carry on, correct and launch more true and meaningful surveys through coming decades for realization of our visions.

This unfinished business is ready to be finished now, through recent efforts in technology and economics. Nationwide, in-depth research has shown that profitable energy systems and production of chemicals from pollutants could employ our entire working force to the utmost advantage of our general economy while providing pollution-free and lasting energy systems. No wonder that our far-seeing and energetic Senator and former Vice President Hubert Humphrey wrote December 9, 1974:

> "Thanks for your letter regarding guaranteed full employment and a need to make this a key element in the platform of the Democratic presidential candidates, I completely agree.
>
> "In fact, I am working very closely with Congressman Augustus Hawkins, and a coalition of national leaders, to promote the notion of guaranteed full employment, I recently intro-

duced legislation to accomplish this objective. I have discussed it with Wilbur Cohen, Leon Keyserling, Burt Gross and several other leading economists and social planners. While there may be some problems with the bill as it is currently drafted, I believe that it is an important way of focusing attention on this vital public policy issue.

"I have enclosed a copy of the *Equal Opportunity and Full Employment Act of 1946* and my testimony on this legislation before the House Equal Opportunities Subcommittee, for your information, I hope you will find them of interest.

"Again, thanks for writing and reminding me how important it is to achieve the full employment goal, a right of our people for more than a generation.

"Best wishes. . ."

After replying and expressing my happiness about his letter, I wrote the Senator again July 5 1975,

"In today's paper a professional political odds-calculator says you are the only one who can beat the Ford-Rockefeller Presidential team. I have known this for months, so he must be right.

"In addition I have known something more important - that you are the only possible president who can get the country moving again. You see the flow of economic variables and how to handle them: Through insured full employment, for example. You personally know the experts who can secure successful implementation: John H.G. Pierson, Leon Keyserling, John Philip Wernette, Emile Benoit (of Columbia) all of whom have been at it for thirty years. Paul A. Samuelson, nobel-prize-winning MIT teacher, writes about such an approach in his principal book. He wrote me he had no criticism of Pierson.

"All these have an understanding wider than just economic. In the energy field, I brought from abroad the Ocean Thermal Difference System which was then demonstrated at the National Bureau of Standards and by three plants of different sizes at the University of California. Today, the National Science Foundation sponsors a full-fledged investigation. This one system may replace oil-produced or nuclear energy and would of itself employ every available hand. There are any number of other urgent tasks. The listed economists understand this and how to operate.

"You have a chance (but with narrow odds) of being nominated by the Democrats and becoming President on the old pattern. Nobody could blame you if you chose this path. But I wouldn't be true to myself if I did not remind you of another possibility which seems to me cleaner and more monumental: You could announce your candidacy for the Presidency on your own program of guaranteed full employment, independently of party lines, which are no more politically descriptive. You might, in addition, announce that you were going to run with no money accepted or spent. Newsmen would come eagerly to your side. Some would scoff, but you have weathered that sort before. You could say that a candidate collecting money jeopardized his independence. Money interests do not necessarily represent the best for the country or for the economy. The courts would have a field day evaluating such a kind of running. I have discussed it with two prominent newsmen. Could I come see you about it?"

On August 8 the Senator cagily responded that he was not going to run for President. His ambition was to stay on in Congress and be as good a Senator as possible. To this I replied per 20 October,

"Your letter of August 8, seen along with James Reston's October 19 column *Humphrey - Happy Warrior*, fits his and Dr. Pierson's and my own dream perfectly. You are even more clever than myself. Sit tight in your Senate seat and let us come to you - just as Norwegians do and always did when choosing a premier and as the Romans did in the old days: They went out into the fields or factories (and sometimes into the Senate) and found a person who had proven through his life to be the kind of person wanted as a leader. And you, obviously, will manage to do it along with the Democratic Party, and follow all the rules, and have no trouble with judiciary interpretations.

"I see you, also, are favoring the Ocean Thermal Differ-ence Energy System which I brought to this country when it was still "a dream", and now top industrialists and university people tell us it is the system for the future: Unlimited supply of free power, easily extractable, excellently suited to our indus-trial base, pollution free, would employ practically everybody available, in this and many other countries. The future is ours again. Greetings. . ."

On October 22 I added a note, inspired by James Reston's ad-vice to preside presidential candidates that, rather than rhetorics they should name a tentative cabinet, to show what kind of leadership they intended to offer. So I asked the senator's permission to play a game, realizing it would be a harmless game, since geographical and other considerations determined formation of cabinets. I suggested as Secretary of State an outstanding economist who has worked and written extensively in the international field, since what we need in this vitally important position is not just a smiling face and some tricks up one's sleeve but understanding of the basic link and tool in international relations: economics. The jobs of Secretary of the Treasury, and "Senior Advisor to the Secretary of the Treasury" and Chairman of the Federal Reserve System would be filled by the various worthy economists quoted in the preceding pages. The Sec-retary of Defense would be a retired expert in defense research and advisor to a succession of Presidents who lately has written vitally about how to insure better overall security and to save unnecessary and even harmful Defense costs.

This correspondence, this whole book for that matter, could be-gin our coming into our own again, more genuinely affluent, more helpful world-wide than ever before - if the reader joins in enforc-ing these policies. If not, all Hubert Humphrey's, the National Sci-ence Foundation's, the University of Massachusetts', of California's, Lockheed-Bechtel's, Pierson's, Keyserling's, Wernette's, my own ef-forts shall not finish this unfinished business.

Appendix

Speech of Hon. Patsy T. Mink of Hawaii
in the House of Representatives
Wednesday, March 1, 1972

Mr. Speaker, one of my Hawaii constituents, Dr. John H. G. Pierson, has proposed a method to resolve the unemployment-inflation problem by amending the Employment Act of 1946.

His statement, "Completing the Employment Act," offers a most provocative approach to one of the most urgent problems facing the Government.

Dr. Pierson, who has a Ph. D. in economics from Yale, served for many years as an economist and a policy adviser in the U.S. Department of Labor the foreign aid program, and the United Nations. He has published three books and numerous articles about full employment. In this article he puts his proposal into the language of legislation.

COMPLETING THE EMPLOYMENT ACT
(By John H. G. Pierson)

In the twenty-six years since the Employment Act of 1946 was signed into law, the country has experienced five recessions.

Even when business has prospered, the central aim of this Act - useful employment opportunities for all those able, willing and seeking to work - has seldom been brought within sight, let alone achieved. Only for three years, in the Korea war boom, has the official unemployment estimate averaged below 3.5 percent of the civilian labor force (dropping to 2.9 percent in 1953 and to 2.5 percent, in seasonally adjusted figures, that May and June). In as many as eleven years it has stood above 5 percent (rising to 6.8 percent in 1958 and to 7.5 percent that July). Earlier bench marks, not entirely comparable, were

24.9 percent unemployment in 1933 and 1.2 percent in 1944 under wartime price controls.

In the long absence of recessions after 1961 the unemployment rate finally dropped to 3.5 percent for 1969 (touching 3.3 percent momentarily early that year), but the statistics somewhat overstate the actual improvement since stricter definitions of unemployment were used as from 1965 and 1967. Then in 1970 the jobless percentage jumped to 4.9, and in 1971 it hovered around, and averaged just under, 6 percent.

Six percent unemployment now means more than 5 million persons. Even 4 percent sometimes treated as though it were an acceptable, goal' would still leave some 31/2 million persons in this country looking for work and unable to find any. Moreover the published unemployment total understates the real extent of involuntary idleness at virtually all times and especially during recessions. One reason among several is that some persons who want to work full-time can only get part-time jobs. Some others eventually become too discouraged to keep on looking and are then no longer counted as part of the labor force; and so - except for less frequent and less reliable estimating - they slip through the statistical net altogether.

A list of the legislative measures enacted or proposed since 1946 to try to cope better with our national economic problems would be long indeed. Many amendments have been offered to the Employment Act itself, keyed mainly to three objectives: (1) Repeated efforts have been made from the outset to have the Act not only promote employment but also restrain inflationary price increases; (2) Lately, since about 1960, it has often been urged that this law should concern itself with our balance of payments as well; (3) There have also been attempts to go back to the more formal kind of "national full employment budget" planning which was originally suggested in 1945-46 but rejected by Congress at that time.

No amendments other than technical or housekeeping ones have ever been adopted, however, and some of the reasons are easily imagined. Many proposals were addressed to section 2, the Declaration of Policy. - Why load the Act with further policy objectives when its first objective was still not being achieved? Again, the "national full employment budget" concept was originally framed in a way that automatically aroused strong opposition by failing to safeguard the private enterprise interest. And all else aside, tinkering with an Act so broad in scope would have seemed like opening Pandora's box. - Where would the modifications end if once begun?

But are the reasons for standing pat still good enough? The need to have our economy function properly is as great as ever. The quarter-century record of failure of the Employment Act as written is more obvious today than before because of the length and peculiarities of the present slump. Indeed we now have not only the doctrine that full employment and price stability cannot be achieved simultaneously but the experience of the simultaneous non-achievement of both. Meanwhile in engineering, for example, scientifically-minded practical people are every day making progress by simply asking "what would be the conditions under which X" (some desired result) "would be achieved?" and then proceeding to construct those very conditions. Certainly the question must be raised whether the arguments against changing the Act are still convincing.

The Answer to this must depend at least partly on whether amendments can be framed that will once and for all complete the Employment Act - make it do what it should, ideally speaking, have done from the start. Can it be strengthened to guarantee jobs to able job-seekers, while at the same time staying clear of irrelevant matters? (To keep full employment from itself causing inflation is of course anything but irrelevant.) Can these things, moreover, be done without prejudging the handling of the touchy public- versus private-sector issue; or changing the traditional relationship between the President and the Congress (as by expecting Congress to rubber-stamp a Presidential spending program or to give the President unduly wide discretionary powers); or interfering in the legitimate concerns of Congressional committees?

It is here submitted that all this is possible, and textual amendments to the Act are offered below to illustrate how. Much the most important amendment and the key to the others is the addition of a new final section 6 to vest appropriate responsibilities in Congress as a whole. However, for the sake of clarity, this discussion will proceed straight through the Act from the beginning.

First, however, a word is needed about what is really at stake, because the arguments over the full-employment issue are often pitched on altogether too narrow ground. In briefest summary:
(1) Involuntary unemployment is destructive of personality.
2) An assurance of continuous prosperity and full employment would weaken the antisocial (usually inflationary) compulsions of business, labor, farmer, and other interest groups.

(3) Racial peace seems impossible in this country without universal job opportunity - the present lack of which is also partly responsible for the alienation of youth, not to speak of the helpless bitterness of many older people.

(4) Getting rid of poverty would be greatly simplified as a result of the cash-income effects of continuous full employment (more paid labor; less chance of exploiting labor by paying substandard wages).

(5) The extra wealth (GNP) which would be created under those full-activity conditions - the staggering amount now wasted through avoidable nonproduction - is needed to help finance programs to meet the problems of the cities, backward rural areas, and the environment generally, including again problems of poverty but not limited to them.

(6) Internationally, that extra wealth would confirm our ability to extend more generous aid to the world's less developed countries.

(7) More (and more fundamental) than that, confidence in our ability to maintain a market adequate for our own full-employment prosperity through domestic policy would substantially deflate our fear of imports and our exaggerated preoccupation with export markets and export surpluses; thus it would enable us to be a "good neighbor" that encourages and helps the less developed countries to shift "from aid to trade" as they become ready for it.

Section 1 of "AN ACT to declare a national policy on employment, production, and purchasing power, and for other purposes" (60 Stat. 23) (Public Law 304-79th Congress) (approved February 20, 1946) merely states that the short title is "Employment Act of 1946."

Section 2 is the "Declaration of Policy." This has received so much attention that it will be quoted here in full, with proposed additions to the text italicized (as also subsequently) and proposed deletions placed within square brackets:

> "Sec. 2. The Congress hereby declares that it is the continuing policy and responsibility of the Federal Government to use all practicable means consistent with its needs and obligations and other essential considerations of national policy, with the assistance and cooperation of industry, agriculture, labor, and State and local governments, to coordinate and utilize all its plans, functions, and resources for the purpose of creating and maintaining, in a manner calculated to foster and promote free

competitive enterprise and the general welfare, conditions under which there will be [afforded] the assurance of useful employment opportunities, including self-employment, for those able, willing, and seeking to work and to promote maximum employment, production, and purchasing power; and opportunities for training, to improve employability; and healthy growth of production, with full, non-inflationary employment and purchasing power."

Comments:

(1) It is necessary to include an assurance of employment opportunity, since that is the heart of the matter. (The rather profuse introductory language of this Declaration might perhaps be pruned a little too without sacrificing vital safeguards, but that is not essential, and the changes suggested here are purposely held to a minimum.)

(2) The concept of "maximum employment . . ." has been a false lead from the beginning. Maximum purchasing power is inflationary. Maximum employment is either inflationary or simply weak ("let's do the best we can"). And maximum production is now more than ever open to challenge as a national objective, both psychologically and ecologically. Hence there is much to be said for rewording the final clause.

(3) The Employment Act is not the place where training programs should be spelled out. As far as policy is concerned, however, there is or should be a national purpose not only to provide employment opportunities for all those able, willing, and seeking to work but also to fight against so-called unemployability; that is, to help anyone, "willing" and "seeking" but not as yet "able," to overcome his or her inability. Hence the end of this Declaration could well refer to that issue too, as here suggested.

Section 3 deals with the "Economic Report of the President." Additional language is proposed for the first subsection in order to give special emphasis to certain recommendations, not now debarred but not explicitly required either, which the Economic Report definitely needs to include:

"Sec. 3. (a) The President shall transmit to the Congress not later than January 20 of each year an economic report (hereinafter called the 'Economic Report') setting forth

(1) the levels of employment, production, and purchasing power obtain-

ing in the United States and such levels needed to carry out the policy declared in section 2, including specifically the minimum and maximum levels of employment recommended in the light of that policy, and the minimum and maximum rates of aggregate personal consumption expenditures deemed consistent with that policy in view of the program of Federal Government purchases of goods and services recommended to be undertaken and the anticipated other demands on the national product;

(2) current and foreseeable trends in the levels of employment, production, and purchasing power;

(3) a review of the economic program of the Federal Government and a review of economic conditions affecting employment in the United States or any considerable portion thereof during the preceding year and of their effect upon employment, production, and purchasing power; and

(4) a program for carrying out the policy declared in section 2, together with such recommendations for legislation as he may deem necessary or desirable."

Comments:

(1) The proposed minimum level of employment (in terms, presumably, of the seasonally adjusted monthly national total reported by the Department of Labor) would reflect the President's view of the correct statistical definition of full employment for the year ahead. This quantity would be derived by estimating the civilian labor force and subtracting the amount of unemployment that seemed to the President reasonable in the light of production shifts, manpower policies, and labor mobility at the time (the allowance for "necessary frictional unemployment"). Apart from labor-force growth due to the changing size and age composition of the population, an effective full-employment policy would no doubt also bring into the picture at the beginning many persons previously not even on record as wanting to work. No need, however, to attempt the impossible. In the transition period from our present excessive unemployment, the President could if he thought best propose moving up to full employment by stages and reaching it in, for example, the second quarter of the second year.

(2) A maximum limit on employment is needed too, as a safeguard against inflation. (Purely as illustration, if the President in some year proposed a mini-

mum of 86.5 million jobs, he might also state that anything above 87.8 million jobs would represent overemployment - too tight a situation in the labor market, with too much upward pressure on pay scales and on total income payments.)

(3) Key importance attaches to also setting limits to personal consumption expenditures (as compiled quarterly, at seasonally adjusted annual rates, by the Department of Commerce), and to deriving this target in the manner indicated. In the first place, since the President would of course state that any expansion or contraction of his recommended government program would imply an opposite change in needed consumer spending, this approach would eliminate the fear that a government commitment to serve as "employer of last resort" might lead to a degree of expansion of the public sector that was unacceptable to Congress. Such a government commitment - such underwriting of the job market - would still be essential, of course; and some consequent manipulation of the level of employment on public works and services would result, in compensation for net "error" in estimating other forms of demand and the employment-generating effect of a given demand. But there would be no inherent one-way bias toward government expansion, no greater probability (if the mid-point between the employment floor and ceiling were aimed at to begin with) of a need to accelerate public works and services than of a need to decelerate them. Hence this approach would remove a basic obstacle to the solution of the problem of making continuous full employment possible in practice.

This approach would also greatly help to remove the second basic obstacle, which is the fear of inflation. While that subject can, best be viewed in a comprehensive way at a later point, it is evident that a firm ceiling on consumer spending (mentioned here, explained in due course) would act as a powerful brake against inflationary demand spirals, especially when coupled with the proposed ceiling on employment.

To return to the computations envisaged. First of all, all the statistical series needed are continuously available. Second, while all the components of gross national expenditures, or GNP, would be used for deriving the needed consumer spending, there is no proposal here that the GNP itself or any of its components except consumer spending should have lower and upper limits set. The suggested procedures do not imply control over private investment decisions, for instance. (Given the permanently high final-product markets implied by the policy, private domestic investment could be expected to continue reasonably high also, with its cyclical swings damped down considerably. In estimating it for the purposes here in view, there might be advantages in choosing a mid-point figure on the diminished investment cycle rather than an actual forecast figure. This would look toward having fluctuations in private construction offset by opposite ex post fluctuations of public works rather than by opposite ex ante fluctuations of private consumer spending.)

This much having been said, the technical estimating procedure may be clarified, at least in outline. Other things (specifically, the sum of State and local government purchases of goods and services, gross private or business domestic investment, and net exports of goods and services) being equal, the needed total of (a) private consumer spending and (b) Federal Government spending for goods and services would remain constant too. ("Needed" here translates into required for a full-employment level of GNP, at a given level of prices.) In point of fact, other things cannot be expected to be quite equal if the ratio of (a) to (b) changes. In particular, certain common types of government spending yield more employment, dollar for dollar, than does more private consumer spending. A substantial program of public service employment would, moreover, have the great advantage that it would help to ease the disproportionately high unemployment among less-skilled and less-educated workers. But differences such as these can all be roughly estimated, just as can the other components of the GNP. Thus, the President would add his optional items to the relatively fixed or unavoidable ones already there and would state what total volume of purchases of goods and services he wanted the Federal Government itself to undertake. He would then specify the level of private consumer spending that in his view would be required to be associated with that much Federal Government spending in order to have, at the price level which he anticipated, an aggregate market capable of sustaining full employment as he had defined it. And no doubt he would also suggest - without needing to have the law say so - a scale of variations of the consumer component that would be appropriate in case Congress introduced variations of the government component.

Here also appears the third major advantage from pegging consumer spending. An increase of net exports has often been sought in the past as a solution for or our unemployment, even though other countries might suffer from the action we took. The proposed approach would turn the problem around, calling for an expansion of the domestic market (via larger consumer spending) when the foreign market (net exports) was projected as declining. Consequently this approach would allay fears of a shortage of markets in the overall sense, and so would help us to maintain a liberal foreign-trade policy based on the widest interpretation of national self-interest.

(4) Part (4) of the subsection asks the President to set forth his program and, if necessary or desirable, recommend new legislation. Although the text here probably needs no formal amplification, the President would clearly be concerned - under this proposal - not only with legislative and administrative measures directly or indirectly affecting the performance of the economy on a continuing basis (welfare reform and antitrust action, for instance) but also with special compensatory measures. The latter would be for use only when that might prove necessary to keep total employment, total personal consumption expenditures, or both from straying outside their specified limits. The subject of contingent, compensatory measures is, however, reserved for later discussion.

Not to overlook the regional aspect of the employment problem - the President's program would certainly not limit itself to questions of national averages. Also dealt with in his recommendations would naturally be the continuing special needs of the country's Appalachias, as well as any unusually severe local job shortages of a more temporary nature brought about, say, by technological change or import competition.

No comment is required on the remainder of section 3. Subsection (b) authorizes the President also to transmit supplementary reports to Congress. Subsection (c) states that the *Economic Report* and any supplements shall be referred by Congress to its Joint Economic Committee.

Section 4 of the Act deals at some length, in six subsections, with the "Council of Economic Advisers to the President." The functions of this three-member Council, established in the Executive Office of the President, are essentially those implied by its title.

Section 5, the last one as the Act now stands, brings us to the "Joint Economic Committee." Here again the text deals largely with matters outside the scope of the present analysis, such as the Committee's composition (ten Senators and ten Members Of the House of Representatives, with the majority party represented by six members in each case), the holding of hearings, the appointment of experts, consultants, and other assistants, the procurement of printing and binding, the authorization of necessary appropriations, and so on. Subsection (b), however, one of the five subsections, is concerned with the vital issue of what happens to the President's *Economic Report*, and here a brief amendment needs to be incorporated, consequential on what comes later. With the proposed addition, this subsection would read:

"(b) It shall be the function of the joint committee -

(1) to make a continuing study of matters relating to the Economic Report;

(2) to study means of coordinating programs in order to further the policy of this Act; and

(3) as a guide to the several committees of the Congress dealing with legislation relating to the *Economic Report*, not later than March 1, of each year (beginning with the year 1947) to file a report with the Senate and the House of Representatives containing its findings and recommendations with respect to each of the main recommendations made by the President in the *Economic Report*, together with a draft Joint Resolution for the consideration of the Congress as provided for in section 6; and from time to time to make such other reports and recommendations to the Senate and House of Representatives as it deems advisable."

Comments:

(1) The process which the Act has caused the President and his advisers to initiate each year by preparing the *Economic Report* should no longer be allowed to disappear in thin air at the end. Rather, if there is to be the practical possibility of assuring continuous full employment, it is essential that Congress as a whole should also assume appropriate responsibilities. Everything hinges on that.

(2) A procedural problem arises at this point because the Joint Economic Committee, in spite of what the law says about its powers to recommend, is not regarded as having the authority to recommend "legislative" action to Congress as a whole. Logically speaking, this Committee, with its detailed understanding of the subject, is clearly the one to prepare the annual draft joint resolution. As an interim measure it might if necessary work with one or more of the other, legislative committees in preparing the resolution for submission to Congress as a whole.

We come now to the decisive amendment that would complete the Employment Act by making provision for nearly all the action required to assure continuous full employment from that time on. This proposed new Section 6 would presumably be entitled "Congressional Action on the Report of the Joint Economic Committee," and could for brevity be phrased approximately as follows:

> "Sec. 6. As soon as practicable after the filing of the report of the Joint Economic Committee, the Congress shall by joint resolution of the Senate and the House of Representatives set forth its decisions with respect to
>
> (a) the minimum and maximum acceptable levels of employment throughout the year in question;
>
> (b) the minimum and maximum acceptable rates of aggregate personal consumption expenditures throughout the year;
>
> (c) the preventive action to be taken by the President if employment should at any time tend to fall below its minimum, or rise above its maximum, acceptable level as defined in (a) ; and
>
> (d) the preventive action to be taken by the President in case personal consumption expenditures should at any time tend to fall below their minimum, or rise above their maximum, acceptable rates as defined in (b).

Comments:

(1) In adopting this amendment Congress would obviously not be comitting future Congresses on the substance of their decisions on the four indicated subjects but only on always reaching some definite decisions on them.

(2) Congress would always have the option to agree with or differ from the President on the minimum and maximum acceptable levels of employment, or in other words on what "full employment" should mean for operating purposes. It might take a different view, for example, of the size of the labor force (the Joint Economic Committee has the help of its own staff experts); or of how much frictional unemployment was acceptable (the President might have considered, say, 3 percent unemployment as tantamount to full employment, whereas Congress preferred 3.5 percent, or 2.5 percent); or of how wide a gap should be allowed between minimum and maximum limits.

(3) The decision on acceptable rates of aggregate personal consumption expenditures would above all settle the public-versus private-sector issue in the way Congress wanted it settled at the time. Suppose that in some year the President's program if adopted would go so far in reordering the country's priorities as to increase not only the overall emphasis on social welfare

fields (health, education, low-cost housing, anti-pollution, and so on) but also the percentage of GNP represented by the government's own purchases of goods and services. The majority in Congress might agree - or go even farther. On the other hand, perhaps the majority would favor maintaining the existing GNP ratios instead. Thus, to illustrate, Congress might some year decide that the acceptable limits to consumer spending would be $765 billion and $780 billion, whereas the President, having different GNP proportions (more heavily weighted on the government side) in mind, had recommended a range of only $745-760 billion.

(4) While decisions under proposed clause 6(b) would thus clearly imply a certain general view of the government's economic role, they would not tie the hands of the Committees on Appropriations, let alone exert any refined degree of control over the elusive question of how much the Federal Government would in fact spend before the year was out. As already noted, the purpose of the pre-announced limits to consumer spending would be quite different: first, to separate the "big government" issue from the full-employment issue; second, to provide, by way of the maximum limit set, a brake against any inflationary upward spending spiral; and third, to make it possible to accept a reduction in our traditional export surplus - since our ability to maintain adequate total markets for domestic output would remain unaffected.

(5) Fundamental to proposed clauses (c) and (d) is that both provide for action that would be made contingent on the showing Of the chosen indicators and mandatory in application when one or both of those indicators began to move outside the Congressionally predetermined range. In other words, as far as these compensatory adjustments are concerned (other sorts of economic legislation are dealt with just below), Congress would begin making the rules in advance and would have a more basic policy-making role.

(6) Under clause (c) Congress would be writing the specifications for a government commitment to serve as employer of last resort. Broadly speaking, that commitment would necessarily entail contingent accelerations and decelerations of public works and services. What would be up for decision would be such things as the exact content of that category for the purpose in hand (with reference, for example, to Federally financed State and local government projects and perhaps private non-profit projects); how to secure an adequate, ready reserve shelf of suitable projects; and the best formula for apportioning accelerations and decelerations by States.

(7) Under clause (d) Congress would have a wide range of options. It might,

for example, decide that, when and if adjusting aggregate personal consumption expenditures should prove necessary, this would be done by temporarily reducing or increasing personal income taxes - and (on the "up" side, at least) by taking some other fiscal action that would comparably benefit low-income groups not liable for income tax. Or, if welfare reform had led to adoption of a plan guaranteeing a minimum income to all families and single individuals as a matter of right, and of a negative income tax as the pay-out mechanism for this, then Congress might decide that the income tax itself (positive and negative) should be the vehicle for all the necessary adjustments. The allowances or negative taxes would in that case be raised, and the positive income taxes lowered, when necessary to increase consumer spending, and conversely the positive income taxes would be raised, and the allowances lowered (but never below their base level), when necessary to decrease it. On the other hand, Congressional economic advisers might consider that variations in consumers' saving could still - even in the absence of booms and slumps - partly frustrate any effort to control their spending by merely controlling their disposable income. In that case Congress might decide on a more direct procedure. (8) For example, Congress could enact a Federal sales tax/sales bonus which would be put on a standby basis to be used only for lowering or raising consumer spending to hold that aggregate within the stipulated limits. As a bonus, when spending was running too low, it would work like a (universal) stamp plan: all buyers of goods and services at retail would during pay-out periods receive stamps convertible (unlike food stamps) into cash at a bank or post-office if promptly presented. As a tax, it would automatically lower the amount of consumer expenditure received net of tax by business, that being then designated the amount required to be held below the established ceiling. Consumer spending could thus beyond any doubt be restrained to any desired extent, any "stubbornness" in spending or saving propensities (and any reluctance to regulate consumer credit) to the contrary withstanding; or alternatively, it could be given a very powerful incentive for expansion. (This fiscal device was first proposed in my communication *On Underwriting Consumption and Employment* published in *The American Economic Review* in September, 1955.) (9) To see, finally, how this proposed unified action by Congress as a whole would mesh with the normal functioning of the Congressional committee system, let us suppose, for example, that the House Ways and Means Committee took up again the general subject of tax reform. While such tax changes as Congress ultimately adopted would no doubt alter the distribution of the tax burden and probably also the level of tax revenue, neither the target-fixing under section 6 (b) nor the choosing of a contingent compensatory formula under section 6(d) would be affected. What almost certainly would be affected is the actual (preadjustment) rate of consumer spending and its likelihood of falling within the acceptable range "of its own accord"; - and hence also the likelihood that the President would actually have to apply the contingent adjustment measures provided for under 6(d).

(10) Incidentally, there would be some presumption that by a kind of feedback effect any unduly large or frequent need to take either type of compensatory action (to adjust consumer spending or to adjust employment) would lead to the sponsorship and passage of improved legislation relating to distribution of income, enforcement of competition and/or regulation of monopoly, or other factors strategically affecting the self-balancing capacity of the economy.

The above-described actions required to effectuate this proposal - first, the enactment of certain amendments to the Employment Act; second, the annual sequences of steps by the Council of Economic Advisers, the President, the Joint Economic Committee, and Congress as a whole would of course need to be supported by operational actions. The proposed approach is broadly describable as Economic Performance Insurance, and the country in taking out that kind of insurance policy could expect to see an "automatic" response to the key signals. But it is important to realize that this "automaticity" could not eliminate the need for decisions at the operating level. On the contrary, Judgment would be called for not only in the recurrent formulation of terms and procedures but also in the execution process.

The agencies to be designated by the President to operate under this law need not, it would seem, be specified in the Employment Act. The only two statistical indicators required to serve as primary action signals are currently prepared by the Departments of Labor and Commerce, as already noted. Perhaps the Labor Department would also be given broad responsibility over accelerations and decelerations of public works and services. Meanwhile the Internal Revenue Service would have a major part to play in administering the contingent adjustments in consumer spending or disposable income, but would work, presumably, in close collaboration with the Department of Health, Education, and Welfare and other agencies of the Executive Branch. Timing would present the big challenge. Postponing all action until the employment level or the rate of consumer spending was already too high or too low to be "acceptable" would breach the continuity of the system before correction could take hold. Then again, after any correction was made, the question would arise as to just how soon (at what point within the acceptable per performance range) the use of the compensatory device should be terminated.

At present the seasonally adjusted monthly employment totals are published some three weeks after the statistical survey - in the early days of the next month; and preliminary quarterly personal consumption expenditures data, at seasonally adjusted annual rates, are published seven weeks or a little less after the end of each quarter. Those time intervals could perhaps be shortened somewhat; in any case, government experts with access to the data can certainly see trends emerging before the results are published. Nevertheless, there must also be considered the further time lag between ordering a compensatory measure instituted and having it put into effect. For example, an immediate acceleration of public works and services is hardly possible on a geographically widespread basis. In signing a $1 billion appropriation bill to create emergency public service jobs President Nixon said on August 9, 1971 that the first group of unemployed should be at the new jobs by Labor Day - nearly a month later. Of course, we neither have nor have had anything approaching either an adequate reserve shelf of public works and services or an adequate system of getting ready to use it; to remedy those deficiencies would be a major project to be undertaken concurrently with amending the *Employment Act* itself.

The best answer to problems of timing would thus probably combine at least the following three elements:

(1) Congress might agree that employment and consumer spending could without prejudice be at "unacceptable" levels briefly - say, for a single reporting period.

(2) Substantial effort and expense should be undertaken to build up an adequate reserve shelf on a nationwide basis, and also to give local organizations the capacity for swift action in carrying out Washington directives in regard both to "last resort" employment and to the fiscal means chosen for adjusting consumer spending.

(3) The Federal agencies in charge should probably issue an "alert" before employment or consumer spending actually went beyond an upper or lower limit, if it seriously threatened to do so. Their staff economists would thus be expected to use a fairly wide range of data and forecasting procedures. Moreover some wrong guesses would inevitably occur, so that some expense

would be Incurred throughout the country in mobilizing forces to meet contingencies that failed to materialize. Reimbursing such expenses would simply be, then, one of the financial costs of maintaining a full-employment system.

A concluding word about inflation. If full employment were, as so often alleged, bound to generate inflation, amending the Employment Act to give it real teeth might have little point. But two recent developments have brought that gloomy thesis into the most serious question - first, the ample demonstration that inflation now tends to occur even without full employment, and second, the not unrelated shift of informed public opinion into favoring an incomes policy of some kind to help maintain price stability. Thus full employment need no longer carry such burdens as do not, properly speaking, belong to it.

More than that, however, it is here submitted that a program of guaranteed full employment along the lines suggested would not only not feed inflation but actually be the best cure for inflation. This is asserted for two reasons in combination. First, the ceilings on employment and on consumer spending that would be imposed under this approach would choke off upward demand spirals almost entirely. That is the built-in "mechanical" aspect. It would limit "demand pull" directly, as already emphasized, and indirectly it would also moderate the wage-demand side of the "cost push" by holding down the prices that make up the worker's cost of living. Second, there is the psychological point that cannot be proved but that should appeal to common sense - a point that would arise from the very fact of the government's readiness to commit itself in this unprecedented way. An agreement on the part of the government to assure a total market adequate for business prosperity, and to assure continuous full employment for labor, should be enough to persuade business and labor leaders to agree to abide by some reasonable set of price and wage guidelines.

Those who blame inflation on the incurable wickedness of Big Business or Big Labor or both often seem unaware of how far the behavior of both has been caused by the malfunctioning of our economy - its cyclical instability combined with secular weakness - the inevitability of which is precisely what needs to be denied. Once the government stood ready to assure continuously adequate total demand for products and for workers, (1) all businesses would have more chance to spread their overhead costs and hold prices down; (2) management in areas of administered pricing could logically give up planning for extra profits in boom times to cushion losses in future slumps; and (3) union leaders would feel less pressure to demand extreme hourly wage rates on the one hand, or annual pay guarantees on the other, to fortify their members against the return of unemployment.

To put this in context - as these words are being written, the country is deep in President Nixon's economic Phase II. Whether this experiment with a Wage Board and a Price Commission will, be followed soon by selective permanent legal controls or by some other incomes policy is impossible to say. But what the government commitments proposed in this article would in any case contribute, when it comes to resolving the ultimate hard-core part of the "cost push" phenomenon, is to open the door as wide as possible to achieving essential results by voluntary cooperation.

Afterword

This archival edition of *Every Willing Hand* has been published as it was originally written in the 1970's, but the information and ideas this book promotes can be transposed to present day events and applied to problems and situations arising in the world today.

With *Every Willing Hand* we see a way to all work together for the survival of humanity. The answers, as Shamcher has indicated, will arise through insight and our human intuition. With yoga and Sufi pathways to develop and evolve the inexhaustible resource of intuition, we will become more able to discern, invent and create the world that is waiting in the wings – all implemented through the connected work of "every willing hand."

Do we dare to imagine an international coordinated effort, similar to the full-scale mobilization of allies at war, that would employ everyone at every level to prevent further environmental destruction, encourage the nurturing of the planet locally and globally, and apply new technologies for the good of all? Do we dare to imagine these efforts linking together as one, while providing employment for all who wish to join in?

Every Willing Hand is a publication of the Shamcher Archives, dedicated to preserving and publishing the works of Shamcher Bryn Beorse. It was previously published by Hu Press, NY, in 1979.

More info at www.every-willing-hand.shamcher.com

About the Author

Bryn Beorse (Shamcher) (1896-1980) was the author of many non-fiction books, novels and articles, covering topics of energy, economics, full employment, and global awareness as well as yoga and Sufism.

Born in Norway, he worked and travelled in over 65 countries in his lifetime, and he eventually settled in the United States. Fluent in several languages, his comprehensive worldview included the inner meditative life as well as the accomplishment of life in the world.

Sent on a UN economic mission to Tunisia in the 1960's, helping to rebuild the Norwegian economy after WWII, Beorse also spent time in exploration, travelling to the Kumbha Mela in India, living as a beach bum in the dunes of Oceano, and going to China at the time of the revolution. A spy in WWII, he was part of the plot to kidnap Hitler. An advocate of the giro-credit economic system, he spoke out against the stagnation of hierarchical organization.

An accomplished yogi and Sufi, Shamcher was instrumental in developing Sufi centres throughout the world, in the tradition of Inayat Khan. He devoted the last years of his life once again to promoting OTEC, Ocean Thermal Energy Conversion, the source of benign solar power from the sea.